The Thorn of Lion City

The Thorn of Lion City

A MEMOIR

LUCY LUM

PublicAffairs
New York

Published in the United States by PublicAffairs™,
a member of the Perseus Books Group.
Also published in the U.K. by Fourth Estate,
an imprint of HarperCollins*Publishers*.

A version of *The Thorn of Lion City*
was previously published by Richwater Publishing.

The names of the author's relatives and other figures who have passed
away are real. The names of the author's living siblings and other
living people have been disguised in order to avoid embarrassment.

PublicAffairs books are available at special discounts for bulk purchases
in the U.S. by corporations, institutions, and other organizations.
For more information, please contact the Special Markets
Department at the Perseus Books Group, 11 Cambridge Center,
Cambridge, MA 02142, call (617) 252-5298, or email
special.markets@perseusbooks.com.

Set in PostScript Linotype Garamond 3 by
Rowland Phototypesetting Ltd, Bury St Edmunds, Suffolk.

Library of Congress Cataloging-in-Publication Data

Lum, Lucy, 1933–
    The thorn of Lion City : a memoir / Lucy Lum. — 1st ed.
      p.   cm.
    ISBN–13: 978–1–58648–436–1 (hardcover)
    ISBN–10: 1–58648–436–2 (hardcover)
    1. Lum, Lucy, 1933– 2. Singapore—History—Japanese occupation,
1942–1945. 3. Family life—Singapore. 4. Singapore—Biography. I. Title.
CT1578.L86A3 2007
959.57'03092—dc22
[B]   2007009383

First Edition

10 9 8 7 6 5 4 3 2 1

In memory of my father,
Lum Poh-mun

My grandmother, Popo

One

'Look at the red-haired devil's air-raid shelter,' Popo said, pointing to our neighbour's garden. 'How clever he is. So different from your father. It is like a house, their shelter, with camp beds and chairs, a wireless and lights. And so pretty outside, with tapioca, sugar cane and all those flowers.'

For weeks my grandmother Popo had told us that we were not to worry: the Japanese would never capture Singapore because the British would turn back the invaders. 'Life will go on as normal,' she said. But there were soldiers on every street, in the shops and the cinema. Every rickshaw had a soldier inside it. There were air-raid drills, and people dug in their gardens, building make-shift bomb shelters. You could tell how big a family was from the size of the mound of soil in the garden. Some of the shelters were like little foxholes, covered with wooden planks, branches and earth, but in our street the red-haired devil's shelter was the biggest and best, and we were jealous. He was the English officer in charge of the police station where Father worked. His wife and children had been evacuated to England and he told Father that if the bombs came we could hide in his shelter with him and be safe.

Father said we did not need a hole under the earth to

hide in. Instead he put the heavy teak table in the middle of the bedroom, then piled blankets and three kapok mattresses on top. He put more mattresses round the sides. He said these would stop the flying shrapnel and the ceiling crashing down on us. 'If the bombs come, you won't need to run outside to our neighbour's garden. You can jump from your beds and curl up under the table. You must have fresh water and biscuits at the ready in your satchels,' he said. 'There will be no time to waste.' When he talked to us about the bombs he was careful not to catch Popo's or Mother's eye. He was frightened of them. They did not like him telling them what to do.

My brothers, my sisters and I looked forward to the air-raid drills. We thought they were games. We five would grab our satchels, as Father had told us, race to the bedroom and dive under the table. It was dark and snug in there and we would play for hours. Sometimes Father would tell us stories about the island his family came from, Hainan, and we would listen and munch our biscuits.

I was seven, and no one explained anything to me. I was frightened of Popo too. Father told me that we should call her Waipo, Outside Grandmother, because she was our mother's mother, not his. But if we called her Waipo she beat her chest and told us she would kill herself. 'This old bag of bones has lived too long,' she would say. 'Even my grandchildren do not love me.'

One day I was brave: I asked Popo who the invaders were and why they wanted to attack Singapore. She went to a cupboard, pushed aside the piles of paper and the tiny red purses in which she kept the dried umbilical cords of her children and grandchildren, and pulled out a great map of the world. It was yellow with age and

2

almost falling to pieces, but she spread it on the table in front of her.

'Listen,' she said, lowering herself into her favourite armchair. 'My mother told me this story when I was a child. The mulberry tree is covered with rich and delicious leaves, which the silkworm likes. This is China,' she said, pointing to a huge pink country on the map. 'It is a country of plenty, like the mulberry tree with its leaves, but it is plagued by starving Japanese silkworms from across the sea.' She rapped her knuckles on the islands of Japan, which crawled across the blue sea towards China. 'The silkworms have hardly any food and their greedy eyes are fixed on China where there is plenty. That is why they attack. To devour us.'

Popo told me of the long history of fighting between China and Japan, about how the Japanese invaded French Indochina, about things I didn't understand then – economic sanctions and oil embargoes, Japan wanting more oil and planning to steal it from Borneo, only four hundred miles to the east, but Singapore was in the way. And she told me of a British man called Raffles, who came in 1819 and wasn't frightened of the swamps and marshes. He had taken control of the narrow strait between Malaya and Java, and borrowed Singapore from the Sultan of Johor. She told me of how the British had come to Malacca and Penang, Labuan and, most of all, to Singapore, and how the Chinese had come too, from Fukien, Swatow and Kwantung, where she and her husband Kung-kung had been born. She told me all of this, and then she spat, 'The filthy Japanese! They have killed many Chinese and we will always be their enemies.'

We lived in British government quarters and our house in Paterson Road was across the street from where Father worked. The house was divided into flats. We had the ground floor and a Malay police inspector lived upstairs with his family. The red-haired devil said they, too, could come into his air-raid shelter if the bombs fell. Our house was square and had wide verandas shaded with bamboo blinds. Inside we had three bedrooms, a sitting room and another room for the servants. In the garden there were hibiscus, papaya, banana, cherry and jackfruit trees, and an oriental henna with leaves shaped like little lances; the Malay women in the *kampung* at the back of our house came to us to ask for the henna leaves and I would watch them stain their palms and fingers for weddings and other ceremonies.

The Malay cemetery, with its lines of numbered round headstones, was next door. It was for Muslims so there were no plants or flowers. From my bedroom window I could see the Chinese cemetery on a hillock across the road, the graves terraced with marble and mosaic. Popo had told me that the richer the family, the more elaborate their ancestor's resting-place; sometimes we played hide and seek among the graves, and when I hid, I would remember the dead all around me and not want to play any more.

A huge durian tree stood at the bottom of the Chinese cemetery; it was the tallest tree I had ever seen, fifty or sixty feet tall, perhaps more. No one dared climb it to pick the fruits, but waited for them to fall to the ground. In season, the abundance of spiny-shelled durians, hanging high in the tree, made people stare. Then the tree's owner would hire two guards to stop anyone helping themselves to the fruit. Sometimes the guards left the tree, and when strong winds brought down the durians, the boys from the *kampung* ran to pick them up. We loved the sweet custardy pulp, and I asked Popo if I could search the ground beneath the tree before the guards arrived in the morning. But she told me, 'We cannot eat fruit from that tree because it is different. The *fei-shui* from all those dead people feed and sustain it and we don't eat the *fei-shui* of dead people.'

The Malay children upstairs wouldn't play with us in the garden. When they came to visit, they would not eat or drink. When they cooked for us we ate their tasty food, and we couldn't understand why they wouldn't eat ours. Father told me about the Prophet Muhammad, and how Muslims could not eat blood or pork, or food that had been offered in prayers. Whenever Popo and my mother went to Chinatown, they would bring back meat and hang it on a bamboo pole in the garden to dry; in the heat, the fat would melt off the bacon and the pork sausages and drip to the ground. Father said the Malay children would not play in our garden because the soil had in it the fat of pigs.

Popo was always talking about the spirits of the dead and the demons who lived in the world below. If we were ill, or there was an accident in the house, she would say it was because one of us had upset the gods. She prayed hardest when she hadn't won at *mah-jongg* for a long time. She would rush to the temple to find out if the gods were angry with her, and pray as hard as she could, then shower them with *shong yau*, oil for the lamp, and burn gold joss paper with the ends tucked in, like tiny ingots. But sometimes she thought her bad luck had been brought about by the spirits from the Chinese cemetery across the road, who came out after dusk to roam free in the upper world. 'They are dangerous and unforgiving,' said Popo, 'not like the gods. The spirits are invisible, but they hear and feel us. When the gates of the world below open, they come out from the earth. Don't pee or spit outside,' she would warn us, 'but if you must, remember to say first, "Forgive me."'

After sunset, Popo would lay offerings to the spirits on the ground at the back of our house near the chicken coop, out of sight of the cemeteries. She would burn silver joss paper, lay out flowers and fruit for the Chinese spirits, and a dozen split coconuts for the Muslim spirits. My brother Beng's job was to stoke the burning joss paper with a metal rod. He liked to pass me the hot end so that I burnt my palm, and screamed in pain. After her prayers Popo would scatter the offerings all over the garden where she said the spirits could find them, but Father worried about our Muslim neighbours. Popo ignored him, and talked of *mah-jongg*, so he would disappear to swim or lift weights, or to the veranda where he had hung exercise rings from the beams. Time and again he would lift himself on to those rings without removing his glasses; when he swung himself back and forth, they would fall off and smash on the floor beneath him.

One day, my father crawled under the big teak table, where I was eating my biscuits, and told me about his life before he came to Singapore. He had been born in Hainan, he told me, the second largest island in China after Taiwan. I had seen Hainan on the map Popo showed me. His parents had owned a fruit and chestnut farm, which his father worked with hired labourers to help him tend the orchards and fell the chestnut trees for timber. His mother had managed the accounts. Father told me that they found it difficult to make a living from the farm. It would rain and rain, and when the river flooded, the expensive fertilizer would be washed from the soil

6

and they had no money to replace it. Sometimes the fruit crop was diseased and they would have to cut down more chestnut trees to sell. Father told me that chestnut wood made good charcoal, which burnt slowly and gave off an intense heat.

He also told me how, shortly after he was born and his mother was still recovering, it had rained for two weeks. The river had got higher and higher, then overflowed its banks and flooded the farm. His mother had watched the garden furniture float away, then the shed where the farm tools were kept, and the little family of piglets they had reared with the sow. When she saw that sow being swept away in the current, she had got out of bed, taken off her clothes and swum after it. But the pigs and the furniture were too far along on their journey to their new home in the sea with the fish, and she waded back to the house. There, she found she was bleeding, so the doctor came and said she would be unable to have any more children.

My grandfather only knew how to be a farmer, but my grandmother was determined that her son should not follow him and did not let him work on the farm. She wanted him to be a government official, or a school teacher. After a day's work, no matter how tired she was, she would read the teachings of Confucius to him. She went to great trouble to buy some books in English from friends who had emigrated to Singapore, and kept them for him as a surprise birthday present. Father said that on his birthday he was in his room writing with a brush pen when he heard his mother call him from the hall. 'Come quick! Come quick!'

When he rushed down to her she was holding out a parcel, and the excitement on her face told him it was a special gift. He took it from her, shook it, squeezed it, and finally tore off the wrapping. The books inside were not new – the covers were worn and the pages thumbed – but he didn't mind because they were picture books with stories in English. Father told me that when he turned the pages of the first he saw pictures of fierce men, with pistols and cutlasses, dragging a boy with them; the book was *Treasure Island*. Another, *Robinson Crusoe*, had pictures of the hero, his dog and a wrecked ship. His favourite was a collection of stories that included 'Aladdin and the Wonderful Lamp' and 'Ali Baba and the Forty Thieves'. As he looked at the pictures, he was eager to read the stories and so, with the help of a dictionary, he began to teach himself his first foreign language.

Work never stopped on the farm, even on the wettest days. One day, when it was raining and the river was swelling, Grandfather was chopping down a chestnut tree. It fell on top of him and killed him. That day my grandmother decided she would leave the island for ever: she would emigrate to Singapore, the Lion City, with her little boy so that he would not be a farmer.

Two

Father told me how that chestnut tree had buried his father in the mud and how his mother's tears had mixed with the rain, and that was why he had come to Singapore in 1919, when he was five. His mother was called Kum Tai, and she was only twenty-nine when the tree fell on her husband. At first Kum Tai was frightened by the hustle and bustle of the city, and as the only work she knew was farming, she bought an orchard of rambutan and mangosteen fruit trees in Nee Soon, north of Singapore, with the money from the sale of her home in Hainan.

Kum Tai named my father Poh-mun, but often called him Po-pui, which means precious seed. Father told us that when he came to Singapore he liked the different people in his new country, and their many languages, which he didn't understand. There were brown-skinned Malay men and women in colourful sarongs, and there were Sikhs from India, who never shaved or cut their hair and wore cloth wrapped round their heads. There were Indian tea-sellers, who carried copper urns heated by charcoal fires on bamboo poles and sold ginger tea or Ceylon tea; some carried rattan baskets full of delicious *roti*. Father would listen to the different dialects, like nothing he had heard in his village in China, and became determined to understand them. He looked forward to visiting the town's bookshops, and spent whole afternoons hiding among the shelves, reading and dreaming.

Kum Tai hired workers for the orchard and a servant to cook and clean. The workers spoke different dialects and she became frustrated when she could not communicate with them: when they misunderstood her instructions, they pruned the trees in the wrong way. She did more and more of the work herself, spending long hours in the plantation. At night the sweet smell of rambutan attracted swarms of bats – the locals called them flying foxes – which would tear apart the soft, hairy shells of the ripe fruit and feast on the white flesh inside. In China Kum Tai and her husband had hired fruit-watchers, who had patrolled all night and slept during the day. But in the new country my grandmother, fearful of the cost of hiring extra workers, protected the trees herself. She walked through the orchards with a lantern and a long stick to scare away the bats, and by dawn she would be exhausted. Father would find her asleep in a chair.

'You are working too hard,' my father said. 'Let me do it, Mother. Let me stay up and frighten away the bats. It is only for the fruit season.'

'Do you know why we left China after your father died?' she said. 'You must not be a farmer here. You must read your books and then, some day, you will be someone. It is the only way for you in this new country.'

One day, while she was supervising the plantation workers, Kum Tai fell and broke her ankle. She had to be carried back to the house. A bonesetter was called, but he did not come, and throughout the night my father heard his mother cry out in great pain. He went to her side to hold her hand.

The next morning, Lum Pang, the bonesetter, appeared

at the farm. He was just five feet tall, very fat, and Father said his grin stretched from ear to ear. Everyone called him Fat Lum. He held his surgery every morning on the pavement of a busy side-street in Singapore. Fat Lum was so fat that the little stool he sat on disappeared beneath his stomach and thighs so that he seemed to be sitting on the ground. He worked next to the tooth-puller, who had a spittoon and cases of extractors and offered only one service: a toothache meant that a tooth had rotted and must come out. When the tooth-puller was called away, he would leave a set of extractors so that Fat Lum could cover for him.

When Fat Lum saw my grandmother's ankle, he busied himself grinding roots, leaves and cacti in his granite mortar with the pestle, and softened banana leaves over his charcoal fire. Then he spread the mixture on the leaves, which he gently wrapped round my grandmother's ankle and tied with fibres from a banana tree-trunk.

Fat Lum was a widower and, like Kum Tai, a native of Hainan Island. He had settled in Singapore many years earlier, and spoke the dialects, English and Malay. Everyone thought he was a very good bonesetter, and while Kum Tai was waiting for her ankle to mend, he came each morning with a fresh mixture of ground herbs and banana leaves. When Fat Lum applied them to her leg, he would help her with the instructions to the plantation workers, in their various dialects, then tell them what needed to be done. For the first time in the few months since she had bought the plantation, everything went smoothly for Kum Tai – especially after Fat Lum had come to work for her, alongside his bonesetting. He asked if she had space for him to live there, rather than travelling from his home in the city. He had no family ties, he said, so there was nothing to stop him. Because my grandmother was a widow, she could not allow him to sleep in the main house: that would have led to gossip and she would have lost the respect of her neighbour. Instead she put him up in one of the outbuildings used for storing fruit.

My father was pleased that Fat Lum was living with them: it would ease his mother's workload. Fat Lum helped him, too, with the dialects. Father loved to follow Fat Lum round the orchards, listening as he gave orders to the workers. Sometimes they would speak Hylam, their mother tongue, but often Fat Lum would use another dialect — the more my father could learn, the less likely it was that he would be a farmer and end up killed by a chestnut tree, as his father had been.

Fat Lum did more and more for Kum Tai and soon he was setting hardly any bones. When he had to respond to an emergency, he would make up for lost time on the farm at the weekend, repairing the house and the outbuildings. Father would gobble his dinner each evening, then rush out to find Fat Lum so that they could sit together on the bench by the duckpond and talk. They would stay there until it was dark when the mosquitoes drove them inside.

One day Fat Lum went to the city and came back, in the middle of dinner, with a stack of books under his arm. Father's eyes lit up. 'Uncle Lum, are these English books for me?' he asked. When Fat Lum nodded, Father stretched out his arms, then remembered his manners and looked at his mother: he did not know whether he should accept the gift. Kum Tai saw the joy in his eyes and knew how much he wanted the books. But she was proud: she did not want it known that she accepted gifts from her workers. On the other hand, she did not want to upset Fat Lum. She insisted on paying for the books, and said that next time all three of them would travel to the city to buy books so that Father would learn not to be a farmer. As they were in the middle of their meal, she asked Fat Lum if he would like to join them. She expected him to say no, because he was an employee, but he said, 'Yes,' with a smile, and lowered his huge body into a fragile rattan chair, which groaned under his weight.

Father had never seen so many English books. 'Thank you, Uncle Lum,' he said, as he leafed through them. 'Can I read with you every day?'

'Of course you can, my son,' said Fat Lum, 'and you must come to me if you do not understand something.'

Kum Tai noticed that Fat Lum had called him 'my son', and was happy that the pair got on so well together.

After that, Fat Lum and my father would sit by the duckpond each evening with the books, and if it began to rain they would shelter in the outbuilding among the crates of ripe rambutan and scarlet, green-stemmed mangosteen. Kum Tai began to worry that her son was spending too much time away from her so, instead of sending meals to the bonesetter in the outbuilding, she began to invite him to dinner so that she could keep an eye on them both. Father would bolt his food and wait for Fat Lum to finish. Then they would sit and read together under the light of the oil lamp until Kum Tai said it was time for bed. Sometimes Father would be asleep already with a book in his hand, and Fat Lum would carry him to bed. Then he would return to Kum Tai and they would chat late into the night.

Kum Tai was alone in a strange country and was grateful for the bonesetter's attention. She thought him a good and honourable man, and feelings for him stirred in her heart. One evening, after dinner, he asked her to marry him. Father was awake in his bed in the next room and waited anxiously for her reply. He knew how difficult it had been for her, alone on the plantation, and since the arrival of the bonesetter her life had been easier. He wanted her to marry again and to sit by the duckpond with Uncle Lum.

Kum Tai and Fat Lum were married at the Chinese Consulate, then had a wedding dinner at a restaurant. The next day Fat Lum told Father that 'Lum' meant forest, like their plantation, and that it would be best if Father changed his name to Lum. Kum Tai agreed that they should all bear the same name, so when Father went to register at the Anglo-Chinese Primary School it was under the surname 'Lum'.

He excelled at school. 'Study hard,' Kum Tai would remind him, 'and get a government job. You must mix with city people, not farmers.' Father told me that he spent his holidays with friends, hiking, camping and swimming in Penang, and that he always worked hard for his exams. 'One day we will sell the plantation and move to the city,' his mother told him. 'But everything depends on you passing your exams and finding a good job.'

Fat Lum took over the running of the plantation and dealt with all the paperwork. Kum Tai was glad that all she had to do was sign the letters. She did not stop guarding the orchards though, and when the trees were fruiting she would walk about with her long stick and a lantern, frightening off the bats. In the mornings she was so tired that Fat Lum could get hardly any sense out of her. 'Why not shoot those flying foxes?' he asked. 'Buy a gun. A few bangs here and there and they will fly away.'

Father told me that at first after Kum Tai bought her rifle things were easier. She only needed to fire a few shots and the bats would be gone for the night. Sometimes she would kill some and take them home to make bat soup. She added medicinal herbs to strengthen Father's weak bladder so that he did not have to rush out in the middle of his lessons.

One night, shortly before the rambutan harvest, Kum Tai was in high spirits when she went out with the rifle to patrol the plantation. As she walked through the trees she thought of the life they would have in the city after her son had passed his exams. The rambutans had turned red and were very ripe and there were more bats than she could ever remember, so she shot many rounds into the night sky. She was under a cluster of trees firing her rifle when, suddenly, there was a thump on the ground and she saw a dark shape a few yards from her. She approached with her lantern and, as she drew closer, saw a dead monkey. Blood was pouring from its chest and its hands were clasped as if in prayer. Kum Tai felt faint and began to tremble. She turned and ran through the dark. 'Aii-ee, aii-ee,' she cried. 'I have killed the monkey god! I have killed the great monkey god! My life is not worth living.' As she ran, the low branches of the fruit trees cut her face and eyes and, Father told me, as we sat under the big teak table, the wounds eventually caused the loss of her eyesight.

Back at the house, Kum Tai knew what she had to do. She took hold of the rifle by its barrel and smashed it on the cement floor, screaming at the evil spirit in the gun: 'Get out, get out, get out!' she cried. But the rifle would not break, so she ran outside and threw it into the duck-pond. It sank to the bottom and was never seen again.

After that night Kum Tai was never the same. She became tense and nervous, and would not go into the plantation. Soon she was unable to work at all and Fat Lum had to take over. She would mumble to herself about how she had shot the monkey god out of the sky, and Father would try to comfort her. 'It's like any other meat, Ma,' he told her. 'They serve monkey at all the best restaurants in Chinatown.' But Kum Tai would put her hands together, showing Father how the monkey's had been clasped in prayer, and she would turn her head and walk away, whispering sadly to herself.

Fat Lum ruled the plantation like a dictator. If a worker arrived a few minutes late he was sacked on the spot, and if anyone was disrespectful he, too, was replaced. Kum Tai did not discuss the farm with him: she had lost interest in it. Father hoped that in time she would regain her health and take back control from Fat Lum, but she did not improve. Instead she began to worry about her only son finding a wife and starting a family.

'Listen carefully, Poh-mun,' said Kum Tai. 'Your father was young when he married me. It is time for you to take a wife. I want to see grandchildren before the end of my days.'

The first time Father saw my mother was at a meeting arranged by the local matchmaker. It happened like this. One day Father and Kum Tai sat at a table near the entrance of a little tea-house in Chinatown and, at the appointed time, a rickshaw, with the hood down, pulled up in front. The matchmaker and the bride-to-be, my mother, were inside.

'She will make you happy, Poh-mun,' whispered Kum Tai, pointing to the girl sitting next to the matchmaker. 'That is Chiew-wah. She will be a good wife, trust me.'

16

Father told me that she was only fifteen, and he had stared shyly at her, unable to speak. The rickshaw stayed for a few minutes, then left. Kum Tai explained that it was not necessary for him to see Chiew-wah again before the wedding, that love was like the wind and would soon blow through them. She talked to him every night about his duty.

The matchmaker negotiated a dowry to be paid by my father's family and a trousseau to be given by the family of the bride. Chiew-wah's mother had discovered that my father's family were well-off and requested ten tables for the guests of the bride's family at the wedding dinner; she demanded a fine restaurant and the very best food. My mother Chiew-wah's trousseau included a set of new teak bedroom furniture, three sets of embroidered linen, a jade bangle, jade and pearl earrings and a thick necklace of pure gold. Father told me that the Singer sewing-machine had been a wedding gift, the very best model, and that was why Mother never let my sister and me use it.

Three

My father told me all of this while we were under the table with the mattresses stacked on top and around it, and I was curled up next to him in the dark, munching my biscuits. Then I could forget the hungry Japanese silkworms crawling towards us with their bombs. I was happy in that place with my father, who had come from the island where the rain had carried the pigs and the furniture down the river to their new home in the sea with the fish.

Father was only sixteen when he was married, and one year later he had his first child, my brother Beng. He told me how Kum Tai had held him in her arms for the first time. 'First Grandson! You look just like your father, my Po-pui,' she said, and tears ran down her face.

'Why are you sad, Ma? Are you not happy with your grandson?' asked my mother.

'I am happy, Chiew-wah, very happy,' she said. 'When I look at my grandson, I think of a time before. I always wanted more children, but after Poh-mun I was not able to have another.' She was lost in thought as she stared at the child in her arms. 'You must not walk too much or carry heavy things, because it will hurt you,' she said eventually. Then she told Chiew-wah how she had swum after the pigs and how it had damaged her womb. 'Don't make the same mistake,' she said. 'You and Poh-mun must have many children, a big family. You must rest. And no housework for one month!'

Father told me that Beng's birth did not interrupt his studies. In fact it made him work harder. He was impatient to pass his exams so that he could get a good job and move to the city, his mother's dream. Her eyesight was fading and she talked all the time about the monkey with its hands locked in prayer. She never left her bedroom: Father took her meals to her there, and in the evenings he would sit with her, reading the book of Confucius that she had once read to him.

Early one morning, in the middle of a thunderstorm, Kum Tai jumped out of bed, got dressed and mumbled that she was going to inspect the fruit trees. Father was at school and Fat Lum had gone to the city on business. Kum Tai stumbled outside in the rain and Chiew-wah, with Beng strapped to her back, worried until Father returned in the late afternoon.

Dusk set in early because of the heavy rain and Father lit a lantern and rushed out of the house. He met Fat Lum returning from the city and explained to him what had happened, then went straight to the tree where the monkey had been killed but his mother wasn't there. He breathed a sigh of relief. Perhaps she had gone to a neighbour's house. And then, in the distance, he saw Fat Lum's lantern. As he ran towards it, he saw that his step-father was bending over a figure on the ground.

Father and Fat Lum carried Kum Tai back to the house, blood pouring from a deep gash on her head. She had fallen and hit it on a stone. When the plantation workers saw her, some left for good because they were frightened of the monkey god's revenge.

Father told me that Fat Lum changed after his mother's death: he wasn't interested in him any more. He made all the funeral arrangements without consulting him. On the last day of the third week after her death, when the prayer rites had been completed, in accordance with the Taoist observance, Father thought the time was right to approach Fat Lum about the plantation and his mother's property.

But Fat Lum beat him to it. 'You can forget about lessons today, Poh-mun. We have things to discuss,' he told my father, as he was leaving for school.

Father was surprised to hear Fat Lum use his name – he always called him 'my son'. 'Can we talk when I get back from school?' Father asked.

'No. You will not be returning here. This is no longer your home.'

Fat Lum went into the bedroom. When he came back, he had with him a pile of documents that proved the plantation had been transferred to him.

'My mother would never have signed those papers if she had been able to read English,' said Father.

It was no use. 'Take your wife and baby and leave. Your mother is dead. We no longer have any family connection,' said Fat Lum. 'Furthermore, the monthly allowance for your education will be discontinued.'

Father told me that he, Chiew-wah and little Beng went to live with Popo, my mother's mother, in her flat in Chinatown – where I can remember living as a small child. There, Mother gave birth to her second child, my older sister Miew-kin; the nurses thought it a good omen that she was born on the sixth birthday of the elder daughter of the King and Queen of England. Popo was a devout believer in Chinese astrology: 'A birthdate that coincides with a royal child cannot be more auspicious for your daughter,' she said to my mother. For once Popo thought an astrological consultation unnecessary. 'What better news can the astrologer forecast?'

When Father talked to me under the table about Popo he would lower his voice to a whisper. She did not like him telling us about those years. I would peep round the mattresses to make sure she was not listening to the stories Father was telling me.

Father explained that Popo paid for my mother's stay in the maternity hospital, and when Mother came home, Popo employed a *pue yuet*, an attendant for the first month. Every day my mother was washed with towels dipped in hot water in which a mixture of lemon grass, pomelo leaves and ginger roots had simmered for an hour. She had to eat special foods to chase away the wind that enters the body after childbirth: ginger roots, dark brown sugar and black Chinese vinegar were heated, then left to mature in great earthenware pots; later, pigs' trotters were added to the mixture, cooked, and served to Mother at every mealtime for four weeks. She was made to drink tea made from roasted ginger roots and boiled black beans, which, Popo said, would prevent arthritis in old age.

The *pue yuet* was the best in the area and Popo paid her well to look after Mother. She spared no expense. Father was not yet working and had no money, so Popo did not consult him. When my sister was born she treated him like a bystander. He offered to care for Beng while my mother nursed the new baby, but Popo would take Beng from him, saying, 'Go away. This is not a man's work.' Then she would mock, 'Poh-mun, how can you stare at books all day and night when you have two children to care for? You should leave school now and find a job.'

But Father had no intention of abandoning his studies after all the sacrifices his mother had made, so he buried himself in his books and let Popo take control of his family.

A year later, just before I was born, he passed his final examinations and found a job as an interpreter. He told me how glad he was to have fulfilled his mother's dream that he would not become a farmer, and how proud he was to be earning money for his family at last.

My grandmother wasted no time in reminding him of what he owed her. 'You are in my debt for life,' she told him, 'and you can never finish repaying me. I took pity on my daughter and grandson. I did not do it for you.'

Father told me that she had worn him down with her insults and demands, and that he had surrendered his first pay packet to her. When he talked about these years I could tell from his voice how sad he was, and tired, and I was afraid of the Japanese bombs coming down on my head, through the ceiling and the mattresses and the thick teak table.

Four

I was the third child and Popo gave me my name. On the day I was born, 19 December 1933, she consulted with an astrologer and chose the name Miew-yong, Subtle Lotus.

I slipped out of my mother in the blink of an eye at the maternity hospital close to Serangoon Road, where the air was thick with spices from the shops where they were milled, and people queued on the pavement, clutching their precious bags of turmeric, cardamom and cumin, grown on their plots of land and brought to the shops for grinding. As they waited their turn patiently, they watched the women squatting over enamel basins of buds and flowers that they threaded deftly into delicate hair ornaments. Undulating rows of floral garlands were draped over poles, the sacred star-shaped champaca among the sweet-scented blooms. Next to the milling shops, goldsmiths sold exquisite jewellery, and fabric merchants displayed layer upon layer of sarees in a tangle of colours. Along the road, tucked away, tiny restaurants served curries, sweetmeats and yoghurt on banana leaves cut into squares.

We lived in Chinatown until I was five. Popo's flat was on the first floor of a three-storey building on a busy tram route, which cut across Chinatown towards Geylang, above a little coffee shop in Tanjong Pagar Road. The flat was divided into small rooms and cubicles, and Father and Mother, Beng, Miew-kin and I had a tiny room at the front. The overhead tram cables hummed a few feet from our window, and as I stood looking out on life in the street below, the trams lumbered by, shooting sparks. How easy it would be, I thought, to touch the cable with Popo's rattan cane. Aunt Chiew-foong, my mother's younger sister, lived in the next room; she had a sewing-machine that she pedalled all day long. Popo and Kung-kung, my grandfather, lived at the back and the three windowless cubicles in the middle of the flat were let, as was the space under the stairs.

To reach the flat we climbed a dark staircase to the large landing area with an altar and the table at which we had our meals. The walls around the altar were sooty with the smoke from the hundreds of joss sticks my family and the tenants had burnt. The flat was gloomy: Kung-kung insisted on fifteen-watt bulbs to save money, but on his birthday he replaced them with sixty watts and, for that day, the flat was flooded with light. In the kitchen there were charcoal stoves for cooking, and in the bathroom a big tub for washing and a toilet, the bowl stained black with age.

Outside, the street was always busy. Workers went to and from the tobacco factory, women struggled with bags of food from the market, hawkers called their wares, and at the tea-shop opposite people met, talked and laughed. I would stand at the window and watch all this for hours, and when I grew bored I would go outside on to the pavement by the door to our flat. Sometimes I would venture further with my father, or one of the tenants, past the tall, terraced buildings with brightly painted shutters

24

and through the tangled streets lined with shops and stalls selling glistening fish, steaming bowls of noodles, cloth of every colour, pots, pans, and songbirds in cages. Sometimes I would be taken to the temple in the heart of Chinatown where my grandmother went to gossip and exchange news with her friends, or to my grandfather Kung-kung's herb stall, where he spent his days telling customers how to treat their ailments and selling them the remedies they needed.

At home Popo would spend hours talking with her *chimui*, sitting in the kitchen as the trams rattled by outside. The *chimui* were her closest friends, her 'foster sisters', and many owned herb shops. Together, they discussed ailments, symptoms and remedies, but they also liked to talk about the past. When she was in a good mood Popo loved to tell her story, and sometimes Miew-kin and I would sit quietly by the women and listen to her talk. We never interrupted: we were careful not to do that.

Kung-kung and Popo had been born in a village in Canton, she said, the capital of Kwantung Province; they married when she was nineteen and he twenty-one. Popo would tell her *chimui* of how she had left her village for Hong Kong in 1911, the year of the Canton uprising, with her husband and his family. They had set up a herb shop in Nine Dragons, and when they had settled in, Popo's mother-in-law had decided to leave her share of the work to Popo. That was how Popo had gained her wide knowledge of medicinal leaves, fruit and roots, and how to use them to treat all sorts of ailments.

Popo said that she had given birth to my mother, Chiew-wah, in the year of the tiger and, two years later, in the year of the dragon, to her second daughter, Chiew-foong. When Kung-kung was not in the shop, he often ventured to the docks to hear tales of faraway countries – America, Russia and Liverpool in England – from Chinese seamen with grey in their beards. He couldn't tear himself away, and on his return to the flat he would grumble to Popo about his long hair, which was plaited into a queue. It had never troubled him until he started going to watch the ships, and now he wanted to look like the sailors: 'They have no queue but short-cropped hair. I want to cut mine off,' Kung-kung said. 'When I bend down it sweeps the floor.' Popo was not surprised when he came home one day with short hair, and it wasn't long after this that he decided to leave Hong Kong and take his young family with him.

As soon as his younger brother was old enough to take over the shop and look after their parents, Kung-kung, Popo and their two daughters boarded a cargo boat bound for Singapore. The island offered many opportunities, he said. They would find good fortune and prosperity there.

My mother was ten and not a good traveller. While crossing the South China Sea, a heavy storm churned the waters and the boat tossed violently. She was seasick and could not keep down any food during the long journey. She stayed on deck with Kung-kung, but every time she felt a little better, the smell of dried fish and meat from the cargo hold below would make her sick again.

Popo would tell her friends how the family had found the flat in Chinatown, and how my grandfather had had to pay the landlord more than he could afford for the lease because so many immigrants were pouring into Singapore. He spent what was left on setting up his market stall selling herbs, the only trade he knew well, but to safe-guard his business he had to pay the *tongs*, the gangsters of the district. They told him that only they could protect him from other stallholders and those who wished him ill, but mainly they guaranteed him freedom from the threats and intimidation of other *tongs*. Kung-kung worked hard and looked to the future: he wanted to expand into a proper medicine shop some day, like the one his family owned. He expected Popo to help him sell the herbs, as she had in Hong Kong, but he soon found that only one pair of hands did the work – his own. Popo told her friends that she would not work on the stall, and she expressed no shame for her failure to behave as a loyal and dutiful wife should; neither did she care that she had not borne Kung-kung sons who would carry on the family name.

My grandfather Kung-kung was a quiet man and paid me little attention, but he let me sit in the corner of his bedroom to watch him smoke his opium, which he did every night after dinner. Kung-kung's bed was his special place, made especially for smoking; there were elaborate carvings on the headboard and on a rosewood panel at the foot. Instead of a mattress, a closely woven rattan mat fitted over the frame. Every night after dinner he would spread over it a piece of heavily stained canvas to catch the tiniest drop of spilt resin. On top he would place a teacup-sized oil lamp and his polished black pipe, which was two feet long with a wooden bowl at one end. When everything was ready he would unwrap the packet of precious opium pellets and place one in his pipe. Then, stretched out comfortably on his side, he would rest his head on a porcelain-block pillow, and begin to smoke.

As I sat watching him from the floor, I would enjoy the aroma of the opium, a delicious roasting smell. Later, when he had finished, he would unscrew the bowl from the pipe, scrape the residue into a container, then painstakingly retrieve every speck of opium that had fallen on to the canvas.

One evening Kung-kung returned home after another hard day's work on his stall. After he had eaten, he hurried to his bedroom and I followed. Sitting quietly on the floor, I watched him make his usual preparations and start to enjoy his pipe. Before he had finished, Popo marched into the bedroom with fire in her eyes. 'Go and smoke in the opium den down the road,' she said. 'I cannot stand it any more.'

Kung-kung looked at her in amazement and I could see that he was angry. 'I have smoked it all these years and now you cannot stand it?' he said, through clenched teeth that the opium had stained brown.

'I am thinking of the grandchildren,' said Popo, looking at me.

'So it's all right for them when the tenants smoke – or will you tell them to go to the opium dens too? Why don't you tell the truth? I'm not stupid. You've made life miserable for Poh-mun, forcing him to hand over his wages, and now you want to do the same with me. I will go to the opium den, but you will regret it.'

Kung-kung never thought of himself as an addict, even though he had smoked opium since he was a young man. 'It is for medicinal purposes,' he always said, reminding everyone that, as a herbalist, he knew what he was talking about. He smoked at home because opium dens were expensive. I heard him complain to Father that the beautiful women who worked there encouraged him to gamble and that this made him smoke more. The dens were dangerous too, he said, and under the protection of the *tongs* who took a percentage of their takings and beat up any addicts who did not pay. Popo knew that the dens

28

were guarded by the *tongs*, who sometimes fought territorial wars; she even knew some of the gang members and could interpret their secret hand signals but, as she told her *chimui* when they discussed what she had done, she was glad to have Kung-kung and his opium out of the house.

After Kung-kung had been forced to abandon his carved bed for the opium den, word spread that he was under the thumb of his wife. He nurtured a silent anger, and spent less and less time at home. Instead he wandered the streets and sat in coffee shops. Some weeks passed and then one day, just after we had finished our dinner, he came out of his bedroom with a suitcase in his hand. 'Take this,' he said to Popo, and handed her a wad of banknotes.

'Where are you going? Where did you get this money?' Popo cried.

'I'm going away and that is all you need to know. Don't wait for me to come back.'

With that, they parted for ever.

After Kung-kung left, my mother went to Trengganu Street where he had had his herb stall to ask the other stallholders if they knew where he had gone, but nobody would say anything. She thought Kung-kung must have asked them not to tell his family. Weeks passed but she didn't give up hope. She returned to the street every day, at different times, trying to find someone who would tell her where Kung-kung was. As she walked up and down, she would think of her journey with her father on the cargo boat, and how the churning sea and the smell of dried fish had made her seasick, and how Kung-kung had taken care of her. She grew more and more distracted and Father became so worried about her that he went to a seamen's club to see what he could discover about Kung-kung's disappearance. When he returned he told us that Kung-kung had met an old friend called Chow, whose ship was in dock for repairs. Chow had told Kung-kung that he had made his home in San Francisco and had offered to get him a job working with him in the ship's laundry.

Popo behaved as if she had done nothing wrong in causing Kung-kung to leave Singapore and his family. With my father's monthly wages and the rent from her lodgers, she had plenty of money, so she spent even more time playing *mah-jongg* with her friends from the temple and with other immigrants who had come to Singapore across the tumultuous South China Sea.

Five

Aunt Chiew-foong was nearly twenty and still unmarried. She had a dark complexion and was less than five feet tall, but she looked even shorter because she walked with a stoop. Compared to my mother she was no beauty, but she liked to smile and show off her decorative gold-capped front teeth. Her voice was high-pitched and shrill, and she would imitate the screeching calls of hawkers, peddling their noodles and chicken congee.

When my mother gave birth to her fourth child, plump and happy with stiff black hair and a chubby face, we nicknamed her Wang-lai. It means 'pineapple' and we thought she looked like one. While Mother tended Wang-lai, Aunt Chiew-foong looked after Beng, Miew-kin and me. She liked to play with us – she was still a child at heart – but Popo couldn't forget that she was still single with no children of her own. She worried that her daughter never had any boyfriends, and I often heard her complaining to her *chimui* about the hard task of finding a husband for her. 'Daughters must be married by sixteen, when they are like flowers coming into full bloom and can fetch large dowries,' she said, 'and parents can have the choice of suitors. At twenty, women are past their prime. Over twenty-five, they are old maids. Then we must pay the costs of marrying them off in whatever way we can.'

According to Popo's calculations with the Chinese calendar, one year had to be added to my aunt's age because she had been born just before the New Year, which made her even older than she was. 'Time is not on your side, you should already have many babies, like your sister,' Popo nagged, day in, day out. 'You wasted many years at school. What work can you do? You can't read or write. You have no luck with matchmakers. How will you find a good husband?'

'Why don't you tell brother-in-law Poh-mun to find one for me, Ma?' Aunt Chiew-foong asked.

My father was persuaded to invite his bachelor friends home at weekends for lunch, in the hope that one might become Aunt Chiew-foong's husband. Sometimes three or four young men would join us, and every week there would be new faces. They enjoyed the food but had no idea why they had been invited. Popo was a good cook, with a discriminating palate, and she had taught my mother and aunt well. Now our Sunday lunches became more and more sumptuous and the menu was planned meticulously days in advance. There were always tasty bowls of thin noodle soup, flavoured with herbs, steamed fish, pork or chicken and sometimes snake, bought live from a stall in Chinatown. After dinner on Thursday or Friday, Popo, my mother and my aunt would begin to discuss their strategy.

'I'm going to make this Sunday's lunch extra special to get a man for Chiew-foong,' my grandmother said one evening.

'No rich bachelors coming this Sunday,' said Mother. 'Poh-mun's invited people who work in other government departments. We don't need anything special.'

'What do you know?' Popo shouted. 'Another son-in-law in the government service would be most satisfactory.'

Recipes were proposed and discarded until Mother

suggested clay-pot chicken. 'You've always liked that,' she said to Popo. 'We'll need chicken, tofu, pork, sea cucumber, Tientsin cabbage, ginger, bean sauce and black vinegar. One taste of the clay-pot chicken and all the men will want to marry her straight away.'

That Sunday the food was the best it had ever been and the guests paid many compliments. At every opportunity my father heaped praise on my aunt's cooking.

One man said, with his mouth full, 'This clay-pot chicken is so good. Better than any restaurant.'

'My sister-in-law prepared everything,' said my father, winking at my aunt.

With all eyes on her, Aunt Chiew-foong rose shyly from her seat with a bowl in her hand and left for the kitchen, apparently to refill it. When she was out of earshot, Father added, 'She's such a good cook. It's a shame I've no brother-in-law.'

Despite the clay-pot chicken, there was no interest in my aunt, and soon my father tired of playing match-maker. Apart from the cost of the food, it prevented him enjoying quiet weekends or going swimming with his friends. In a rare moment of defiance, he stopped the lunches altogether. But Popo did not give up hope. She had consulted a fortune-teller who had told her, 'When the time arrives, Chiew-foong will marry a good, caring husband.'

Then, unexpectedly, one of the bachelors who had attended a Sunday lunch approached Father and asked for Aunt Chiew-foong's hand. He was called Cong and was a government employee from the Municipal Department of Public Utilities. Father was dismayed. 'He's short, balding, and has a squint that makes me uneasy,' he said to my mother. 'He never meets my eye.'

'Why did you invite him to the house, then?' Mother asked.

'I had no choice. Your mother forced me to consider any man as a husband for your Chiew-foong,' Father replied.

But Popo had her eye on Cong and confided to my mother that she did not mind his odd appearance. 'All that matters is that I will gain face when my *chimui* find out where my second son-in-law works.' With a toss of her head, she added, 'They will be so envious. None of them has any family in the government service, but two members of mine will be.'

In view of my aunt's age, Popo did not demand a dowry and insisted that the pair marry as soon as possible: she was relieved that my aunt was soon to be off her hands.

Aunt Chiew-foong and Cong married and moved into his house in Rangoon Road, a few miles from Chinatown. After their honeymoon, Popo allowed them time to settle in, then made her move. One morning, she packed a bundle of clothes and set out, intending to spend a few days with my aunt: she said she wanted to get to know Chiew-foong's blind mother-in-law who lived with them – but really she wanted to test the water, find out if she could get my aunt's family under her thumb as well. She returned the same day, tight-lipped and ill-tempered. It wasn't until some hours later, after much snorting and cursing, that we found out what had happened. At the midday meal Aunt Chiew-foong had served Popo a bowl of rice congee and a small saucer of pickled sour greens left over from the previous night's dinner. Popo had eyed what was placed in front of her in disbelief and asked my aunt what kind of food they were having.

'Teochew,' Aunt Chiew-foong said apologetically. 'I have learnt to prepare their kind of food and to keep to a very strict budget. My husband and his mother don't believe in eating as much as we Cantonese, and I am given enough money each day to buy one meal at the market. I must have meat on the table for dinner.'

'So, Poh-mun was right about your husband,' said Popo, sniffing the congee. 'Yesterday's leftovers.'

'I have hardly anything for myself, Ma, so I have to pocket a few cents from the housekeeping for my daily stake on the *chap-ji-kee*,' Aunt Chiew-foong moaned.

She was addicted to the lottery. She had a cigarette tin that contained the numbers one to twelve written on small squares of paper rolled into little tubes. That tin went everywhere with her. Whenever she came across burnt-out joss sticks at the foot of a tree, a bush or at the corner of a street, she took that as a sign to ask for numbers. She would kneel, if it was a fine day, or squat, if it was wet, then mutter a prayer, and shake her tin until two numbers fell out, which she would scribble down. Her favourite place to consult the tin was by the pond for rescued turtles at the temple, near the market in Balestier Road. If she struck lucky, she would celebrate by going to the stall that served turtle soup. She kept a record of each day's draw in a length of red paper rolled up like a scroll.

My aunt told Popo that if there was nothing left from dinner the day before, she and her mother-in-law would have plain congee, with a sprinkle of soy sauce, for lunch but she insisted, miserably, that she was content and adjusting to married life.

When my aunt admitted that she had no say in how the family's money was spent, Popo's hopes of staying for a few days and taking control of the family were dashed. It was hardly likely that her second son-in-law was going to part with any of his wages. Still, she was curious about what he did with his money. My father had a large household to feed, and my new uncle earned almost as much as he did. She decided that as a bachelor he must have saved a large amount. She began to press my aunt for the truth about her husband.

'Is he gambling?' she asked. 'Does he go to prostitutes? What does he do with his money?'

Finally Aunt Chiew-foong lost patience. 'Enough,' she said. 'He never goes to prostitutes. We go to bed early every night because he wants a fat son quickly.' Then, in a hushed tone, she added, 'I wouldn't dare ask him for money but he talks about it with his mother. She has a lot of gold jewellery.' She nodded towards her mother-in-law's room and whispered, 'It is hidden under her mattress and she never leaves her bed.'

'Why? Is she lame?'

'No, only blind. The jewellery keeps her in bed. She is afraid to leave it unguarded.' Aunt Chiew-foong told Popo that as her mother-in-law never left her bed, her legs had become weak. She took her mother-in-law's meals to her and the woman ate them leaning against the pillows. She wouldn't even take a bath, but was wiped with a wet towel as she lay on her bed. Rather than go to the toilet, she used an enamel pot.

'My husband used to pay someone to come in to help a few times a week, but he sacked her after we got married. Emptying the pot and cleaning her every morning is my duty now,' said Aunt Chiew-foong.

Popo shook her head. 'How can you do this without complaining?' she scolded. 'Aiii-yah, after all the trouble I took to find you a husband, you are a servant to a blind old woman.'

Six

Three years before the starving Japanese silkworms would begin their deadly journey across the sea to Singapore, we moved from Popo's flat in Chinatown to a two-storey house in the Tanglin area of Singapore. Father was doing well as an interpreter and thought that now he could afford a house for his family he would escape Popo. But she decided to let her flat and come with us.

Our new house seemed full of light after the gloom of the flat in Chinatown. Downstairs we had a sitting room, a dining room and a kitchen. Half of the kitchen was open to the sky: that was where we did the laundry and where we ground soaked glutinous rice into the flour that we used to make sweet dumplings. Outside our front door, I would watch passers-by, and families sitting and talking outside their houses. Tanglin was different from noisy Chinatown where people pushed and shoved, chattered loudly in different dialects, and the smelly open drains were always filled with stagnant water and rubbish. The house stood on Emerald Hill Road, which snaked up to meet Cairnhill Circle, and in the afternoons piano and violin music drifted into our house from the children next door. On the pavement boys and girls played badminton and marbles.

Our neighbours in Tanglin were Chinese but dressed

in Malay clothes. They spoke Malay and English, but only a few words of Cantonese. The women wore colourful sarongs and the long-sleeved *kebaya*, made of voile and embroidered along the edges and the cuffs. In place of buttons, a *krosang* – three long gold pins linked with a fine chain – held it together at the front. On their feet they wore multi-coloured beaded cloth slippers, and it wasn't long before my mother and Popo discarded their clogs for a pair each.

We discovered from our neighbours that they were 'Straits Chinese' or Peranakans, which means 'locally born'. Their Chinese ancestors had settled in Malacca, one of the four British Straits Settlements; the men were known as *baba*s, the women as *nyonya*s. Popo said it was strange that a Chinese person could not speak Chinese. Over the centuries the Peranakans had adopted the culture and language of the Malays; my mother and Popo noticed that the *nyonya*s were polite and refined, unlike their own women friends.

My father's office was close by, so he no longer had to cycle to work early in the morning. Instead, he walked through the leafy streets, and I would watch him set out each morning, his black hair gleaming with Brylcreem, combed straight back with a side parting; he wore a crisply starched white shirt and trousers. He enjoyed his job, but his interest in books and languages did not die away. He bought books all the time, regardless of the cost, and paid for them in monthly instalments, building up a small library at our new home. He stamped each one 'Lum Poh-mun Library'. There were books on language, history, psychology and the classics, and one shelf was filled with paperback novels. I would often see my father reading books like *The History of the Roman Empire*, or the five classics: *Changes*; *History*; *Poetry*; *Collection of Ritual*; *Spring and Autumn*. He told me there was so much wisdom in their pages that he could never finish learning from them. His favourites, though, were the *Four Books* of Confucian literature – the only ones he had that his mother had brought from China. He told me that reading them reminded him of Kum Tai, who had read them to him on their farm, where the rambutans and the scarlet mangosteens had grown. From them he had understood the value of learning, the importance of integrity, sacrifice and duty, and that human nature tends to be good.

Popo still ran the house and my mother did not dare challenge her. Father tried to insist that his wife should have his wages but did nothing when she handed it to Popo. With the family money in her hands, Popo dismissed the cleaner, who had come in for a few hours in the morning, and hired a live-in servant to do the washing. Father said that the real reason Popo had taken her on was to impress the neighbours.

Sum-chay belonged to an association of professional servants, known as *mah chay*. They looked down on other servants who did not have their special training and would carry out only certain duties. They wore black trousers and white Chinese blouses, and we called them 'the black-and-white snobs'. Sum-chay made it clear at her interview that she would not cook or look after children. Although she was in her early forties, she had never married and didn't like this to be mentioned. We children called her by her name followed by the respectful 'Older Sister', and after a while she softened towards us and would sometimes keep an eye on my younger sister Wang-lai while my mother was playing *mah-jongg* with her friends. Every festival day she left our house and returned to her lodgings in the *coolie fong*, where all the *mah chay* would congregate, to celebrate with her fellow professionals.

One evening at the house in Tanglin I caught a chill after I had spent too long bathing in cold water. Hot water was a luxury in my family, and we only had it when we were unwell. My cold had persisted for more than a week and I developed a burning fever. I did not see a doctor as my grandmother never allowed us to use Western medicines: she took charge of our health and had a cure for every ailment. Bottles of dried herbs lined the kitchen cupboards, alongside jars of birds' nests, lotus roots, dried bees, lizards, sea-horses and cockroaches. Some, like the sea-horses, were added to soups and stews as a health-giving ingredient; others, like the many bitter herbs, were for medicines. Whenever we were ill, Popo would point at several jars in turn and Sum-chay would take them down and put them on the table. Then Popo would take a handful from one, a pinch from another, mix the herbs on a bamboo tray and tip them into a pot for boiling. Some of her treatments were simple: if a rash appeared on someone's skin, she would say it was caused by spiders crawling over it in the night and would soak dried orange peel in water, chew it to a pulp, then paste it over the rash. Her concoction for my fever was made up of nearly twenty herbs, insects and animal parts, simmered to a black, glutinous soup. I swallowed it obediently, trying to ignore the horrible smell.

Then Popo said I needed a treatment called *mungsa*, which means to 'draw out the sand'. My heart sank. She had done this to me before and it had been very painful. I put on a cheery face and lied: I felt much better, I said. Popo was not deceived. She summoned Sum-chay and told her to hold me down on the bed. She dipped her fingers into a bowl of salted water and began to pinch me, starting at my neck and moving gradually over my chest, my waist and along my ribs to my armpits. I screamed and kicked, but Sum-chay held me fast and Popo kept up the pinching for more than an hour. When she had finished my skin was red and sore.

I knew that for seven days after a *mungsa* treatment I would only be allowed sweetened condensed milk, soda biscuits and fruit, and prayer water from the altar mixed with specks of ash from burnt joss sticks. I would have to embark on this regime the next morning. When day dawned, my fever had not subsided despite the bowl of herbal brew. 'It serves you right for playing with water, Miew-yong,' my mother scolded, and as I lay there I remembered how Mother and Popo doted on Beng when he was ill. As my fever worsened Father became very worried about me, but Popo forbade him to call a doctor. He watched me anxiously, but when I looked up at him his face swam and I wondered who he was. He pleaded with Popo to try something else and finally she prepared a different remedy with rhinoceros horn. As she squeezed open my jaws and forced the liquid into my mouth I heard her scold, 'Don't spit it out, Miew-yong. This medicine is very expensive.'

Popo was worried, not for me but for herself. She was concerned that I would die and she would be held accountable, but she was still determined not to call a doctor. My mother followed her orders and together they made sure my father did not find out that I was danger-ously ill. They massaged me with pungent red-flower liniment and waited. Two days later I woke with a burn-ing sensation all over my body and began to choke at the suffocating scent. My mother was standing next to my bed. I looked up at the woman from whose body I had come, in the blink of an eye, into a world fragrant with a hundred spices, and she gazed back at me with no joy in her eyes. 'Are you hungry?' she said flatly.

A few weeks later my mother had her fifth child, a son. When he arrived, he did not cry until the doctor had held him upside-down and smacked his bottom. Popo said it was a sign that he would grow up to be stubborn. Father said she was happy to have a second male grandchild, after three girls, and she carried him in her arms whispering her pet name for him, 'Little Cow'. 'Sai-ngau, Sai-ngau,' she would say, 'you will grow up to be big and strong.'

Seven

As my father's grasp of dialects and languages grew, so did his wages. When I was six we moved to Paterson Road, opposite the police station run by the English officer, the red-haired devil. As soon as I saw it I loved that big house, with its many windows and wide verandas. The first thing Popo did when we moved in was call in the *feng-shui* master to inspect it. He arrived wearing a Chinese jacket and looked very wise. For nearly an hour he spoke with Popo and my mother, pointing from time to time at a list he had placed in front of him on the table. On it were the names of each member of our family with the time, date and name of the animal year in which each of us had been born. I was curious about what he would do next so when he went out into the garden I followed him. I watched him take out of his jacket pocket a small, octagonal block of wood carved with elaborate decorations and with a compass set in the centre. With outstretched arms he held it out, turning in various directions, and mumbled, 'Too many tombstones, too many tombstones.' With a frown, he replaced it in his pocket, took out a piece of paper, made some notes, then walked to a different place and did it again.

While the *feng-shui* master made his calculations Popo walked round the garden, followed by the gardener, to look at the flowers and fruit trees. In the far corner a bush of mauve bougainvillea had been trimmed into a ball, and was surrounded by orange bird-of-paradise, mother-in-law's tongue, gladioli and spider orchids. Gladioli and spider orchids were Popo's favourite flowers for the altar and she told the gardener to put plenty of cow dung on the beds where they grew. When she got to a huge cactus, with flat fleshy stems and deadly needles, she said: 'Ah, palm of spirit. How useful. I won't have to travel to Chinatown for dried ones now.' She used it to treat the sole of the foot for aches and pains. She would clip off the spines, roast the stems on charcoal and lay them on newspaper. The patient would stand on the hot cactus flesh while it drew the unhealthy wind from the body.

There was another useful tree in the garden, the papaya. Popo did not like the fruit, but she used the leaves when she made a stew of pig's stomach, garlic, tofu and mustard greens in dark soy sauce. She used them to scrub the pig's stomach and remove the lining of slime and the nasty smell. We often ate pig-stomach stew. When Popo and Kung-kung had arrived in Singapore with little money, she had searched for the cheapest food and discovered that Europeans, Malays and Indians did not eat pigs' stomachs, which could be bought for next to nothing. Of course, she never served such cheap food to guests.

When the *feng-shui* master had finished in the garden, he returned to the house and went from room to room, pointing his compass. I wanted to follow him and watch everything he did, but one glare from Popo told me to stay where I was. I wondered whether he had come to cleanse the house of the spirits from the cemetery, but when his inspection was complete, he sat with Popo and told her that he had calculated the lucky date and position for the setting of the altar, then wrote a list of other things Popo had to do around the house so that we would enjoy the beneficial effects of *chi*. After he had gone Popo followed his instructions to the letter.

I found that by climbing over the verandas I was able to get in and out of the house without using the front or back doors, which meant I could come and go unnoticed. While my brothers and sisters stayed at home, I would sneak off to the police-station courtyard to play with the policemen's children. The station stood on two acres of ground at the corner of Orchard Road and Paterson Road. The main building was a typical two-storey colonial-style structure, bordered by verandas on all sides. The charge room, cells and some small offices were on the ground floor, and upstairs the offices of senior policemen and the administration staff, including my father. The red-haired devil's room was the largest, and just outside his veranda a Union flag fluttered on a long pole. Apart from the main building, there were living quarters for about sixty policemen, the prisoner interrogation rooms, the canteen and the recreation hall. In the middle, screened from public view, was the quadrangle where the policemen had their daily parades and drills.

When the drills were taking place, children were not allowed in the grounds, so I would watch from my friend's house close by. As I looked at the policemen, sweat dripping down their foreheads and drenching their shirts, I wondered why they wore such warm clothes for their parades. Eventually I learnt from Father that they had to wear British uniforms – bluish-grey shirts, khaki shorts, knee-high woollen socks and woollen berets.

When I was not at the police station or playing in the garden I would wile away my time on the veranda, watching the lorries pass with their loads of tin, rubber or timber on their way from the plantations in Malaya to the wharves where they would be loaded on to ships for export to Britain. I could always tell if a load of rubber had gone by as it gave off an unpleasant chemical smell that stayed in the air for a long time. The timber lorries carried huge logs held together with a few ropes, and a man sitting precariously on the top log. I thought those men deserved extra wages for being so brave, but my father told me they sat on the load because they had no choice: they needed the work. One day, walking home with my father, we saw a timber lorry brake suddenly and swerve to avoid colliding with a car. As it screeched to a halt, the man on the top log was thrown on to the road and, a split second later, crushed to death under the load of timber that followed him.

With more money and a big house to show off, my grandmother and my mother began to transform themselves. They invited old and new friends to play *mah-jongg* and for meals, and we had visitors almost every day. When Father returned from work, he had to smile at people he hardly knew. My mother stopped doing housework and caring for us to spend most of her time attending to her makeup and going out with her friends. She would see our former neighbours from Tanglin, Mr and Mrs Khoo, and together they would go ballroom dancing and never missed a Sunday tea-dance. She bought a gramophone and invited them to our new house to practise the waltz, the quickstep and the tango. She urged my father to learn, but ballroom dancing was not for him, although he joined in to humour her.

On most Friday evenings two square tables on the veranda were wiped down so that my parents, Popo and the same five friends could play *mah-jongg*. I was already an expert at setting the *mah-jongg* tables but although I felt I could play as well as they did, I was never allowed to. First I lined a table with five or six layers of brown paper to lessen the constant noise of the solid white bricks knocking against each other. Then I poured out the 144 little bricks and left them for the players to 'wash'. Next I counted the chips needed for each player and placed a set before each chair.

The atmosphere at the two tables was very different. At my father's there was quiet, cheerful conversation and analysis of the play. At Popo's, there was loud chatter and the slamming of bricks as the game went on. When Popo, using all her ingenuity to outguess her equally skilled opponents, mistakenly gave away the one brick needed by someone else, she would excuse herself to 'wash away' the bad luck: she would visit the lavatory and wash her face, then light joss sticks at the altar and pray for the return of good fortune.

We were allowed to stand behind the players to watch them select and discard the bricks. Miew-kin and I had to empty the ashtrays, which Popo and some of the other chain-smoking players soon filled again, and refill their cups with black coffee. Beng would sit beside Popo. The games went on for four hours; sometimes the players would break for dinner, and carry on afterwards until early morning.

The number of guests made extra work in the house and Popo engaged a cook. Dai-chay came from the same *coolie fong* as Sum-chay and knew her own value: she stated at her interview that she would do no housework and would shop where she pleased. She was short, with enor-mous buttocks, breasts that hung to her waist, and a deafening voice. Before she agreed to take the job, she strode about our house to inspect it. As we soon discovered, she detested children and took much pleasure in telling tales about us to our parents and Popo. We were forbidden to enter her kitchen without her consent to get drinks and snacks.

Until now Popo had collected the rent every month from her tenants, but now that she had a successful son-in-law and lived in a big house with an experienced cook, she was too proud to do it. Instead she paid her friend Tai-pow Wong, whom everyone called Gasbag Wong, to collect it and deliver the money to her. Popo and Gasbag Wong had been friends from the time when they had first been neighbours in Chinatown. Gasbag Wong was a go-between, doing deals and running errands for a living, and knew many people. Sometimes she helped drug addicts and debt-ridden gamblers to sell their children. Boys were usually reserved before birth by families who had no sons and were willing to pay large sums, but girls were readily available and sold as *muichai*. Although this was against a law introduced by the British, the trade in girl slaves was widespread in Singapore.

On one of her visits Gasbag Wong arrived with a big smile. She normally came alone at the end of each month to deliver the rent money, but this time there were three girls with her, between ten and twelve years old. They looked pathetic and frightened. There were holes in their clothes and they were not wearing shoes. Popo handed a roll of money to Gasbag Wong and ordered them to kneel. Then she said, 'You must be obedient. If you run away, you will be severely punished and your parents must pay back a lot of money.'

Popo's family in China had owned *muichai* rather than

48

employ servants and she was happy to disobey the law. In the households of their owners the *muichai* lived in fear and drudgery. They could be sexually assaulted, beaten, given away to other families or sold by their owners as wives or prostitutes. They were paid nothing and wore their mistress's old clothes. One of the most distressing ordeals for a *muichai* was to be sent back to her parents if she was disobedient. The parents were usually so poor that they would refuse to accept her for fear of having to repay the money they had received from selling her into slavery.

While the girls were kneeling, our cook Dai-chay walked into the room. She looked at them, sniffed the air and said to Popo, 'How can I cook with such a foul smell coming into my kitchen?' It was clear that they had not washed for some time so they were ordered to the bathroom to bathe and have their hair trimmed, then told to try on some of my mother's old clothes. The blouses were taken in, the trousers shortened to fit, and then they were summoned before Popo. The transformation was remarkable. Two of the girls were cousins and their names were Lai-yuen and Lai-pin. But Popo did not like the first part of their names, Lai, meaning 'to look askance', so she changed it to 'Ah', renaming them Ah-pin and Ah-yuen. The other girl was Yan-fok.

Popo chose Ah-pin as her personal maid because she had a pleasant face and would wash and iron Popo's costly silk clothes. Yan-fok had to do the menial work and was at the beck and call of the household, including Sum-chay and Dai-chay. The *muichai* worked non-stop, hurrying to answer every call in fear of a beating or a knuckle round the head and they were not allowed out on their own. Neither were they given time off to visit their families.

49

After many weeks of learning how to do the housework, Ah-yuen was sent to Aunt Chiew-foong, who by now had had her first child and was expecting a second. My aunt said that her husband Cong would not waste money employing a servant, but he had no objection to accepting a free *muichai* who could take his blind mother her meals, empty her enamel pot and clean her as she lay on her bed, day after day, guarding her gold jewellery. Before she handed over the *muichai*, Popo was careful to point out to my aunt and uncle that Ah-yuen would continue to remain her property and only she could decide her ultimate fate.

Eight

Not long after the *muichai* arrived, my mother had her sixth child, a girl. My sister, Miew-lan, was premature and underweight. Mother was disappointed that she wasn't a boy and refused to breastfeed or care for her when they returned from the hospital. She engaged a live-in *amah* to look after her but the *amah* was young and inexperienced. My father had strong misgivings about employing her because my sister, who weighed no more than four pounds, was so tiny and fragile.

'This *amah* has never looked after premature babies. Can she be trusted to care for one so small?' Father asked.

'Well, I'm not going to nurse her. If you don't trust the *amah*, you can look after her yourself,' Mother replied.

As she had done after each birth, my mother washed every day in fragrant water and ate the specially prepared pigs' trotters at every meal. Most of our Chinese relatives and friends were superstitious and considered a house unclean until a new baby was a month old. My mother was impatient for the cleansing ceremony to be over so that her friends could visit again. She spent the evenings before bedtime leafing through the calendar, sighing, 'I wish tomorrow was Miew-lan's full month.' When at last that day arrived, the ceremony was performed. Sprays of leaves from the pomelo tree were added to the baby's bathwater and Miew-lan was rubbed with them to purify her and bring her luck. My mother dipped her own hair and body in the same water and then we sat down with some friends to eat pig's trotters. After the meal the guests were sent on their way with hard-boiled eggs for good luck, the shells dyed bright red.

The next morning, after breakfast, my mother sat for an hour in front of the huge circular mirror and put on her makeup. Miew-kin and I were fascinated by the collection of perfumes, lipsticks, nail varnishes, face creams and boxes of powder that were neatly arranged on her dressing-table, but we knew better than to touch any of Mother's belongings. If we did she said she would burn our fingers with a lighted wick. We would stand on the threshold of her room, as though held back by an invisible barrier, and watch her transform her face. Our fingers itched to reach out and play with a lipstick or perfume bottle. Later that day my mother had her Shanghainese tailor come to the house for fittings. The Shanghainese were regarded as the finest ladies' tailors; my mother's hand-embroidered cheongsams were trimmed with piping and she wore them with matching shoes.

After the birth of Miew-lan my mother left Popo in charge of us. She was very strict and always had a cane by her side at mealtimes. We were constantly reminded that children 'should not have plenty of mouth'. If my elbows rested on the dining-table or were spread too far apart while I was holding my bowl and chopsticks, she would strike them with the cane, and did the same to my sisters. When my brothers made the same mistakes, they were left alone.

Popo would fill our bowls with food and we could not leave the table until we had eaten every scrap. I preferred the Malay food of vegetables, anchovies and beans, which I was sometimes given at friends' houses, to the oily Chinese meat. Sometimes I would look in dismay at the food in my bowl and make an excuse to leave the table without finishing, but Popo would see this as a temper tantrum and beat me.

Not long after we moved to Paterson Road, when I was seven, I started school. My grandmother would wake us early each morning and Miew-kin and I would get ready. I would put on my white blouse and Yan-fok would help me tuck in my cotton trousers, which we wrapped round my waist and tied with a sash. Then she would tie my shoelaces and I would join my family at the breakfast table. We had bowls of rice congee topped with chopped fried breadsticks or piles of steamed dumplings. After breakfast two red-painted rickshaws would arrive outside the front door. Beng would climb into one and Miew-kin and I would get into the other. The rickshaw-pullers, in Chinese jacket, short trousers and straw coolie hat, would take us to school where we would learn to read and write in English, practise arithmetic and sing songs.

Miew-kin started at the school a year before I did and I had only been there a few days when I got into trouble. At mid-morning we had tiffin, and Miew-kin always spent her break with a rich girl who was the granddaughter of one of Popo's friends, a woman whose husband was the biggest importer of herbs in Singapore. This girl was always accompanied by a servant, who carried her metal tiffin box. Once the girl had finished eating, she would offer Miew-kin the rest of her food. When I began at the school I would sit with them during tiffin and eat some too. One morning, as we waited for the girl to finish

53

eating, I decided I did not want to eat her leftovers. I pulled Miew-kin away and said, 'Let's not eat – we don't want it.' Then I turned to the servant and said, 'We are not beggars. Why must we wait until she has finished? Why can't we eat at the same time?'

When we returned home from school at lunchtime, Popo was waiting for me with her cane. The servant had told her mistress what I had said and she had stormed round to speak to Popo. 'Why did you make trouble?' Popo shouted at me, as I struggled in her grip. 'Look at your sister! Now she will have no food.'

As Popo beat me I thought defiantly, I don't want to eat that food. No matter how much you beat me I'm not going to eat like a servant!

After that Miew-kin's friend never offered her leftover food to us again and instead we were sent to school with two cents each to spend in the 'tuck shop'. It was a collection of stalls selling home-made cakes, vermicelli, fried noodles, mixed nuts in paper cones made out of the pages of an exercise book and, best of all, chocolate milk from England, which I loved to buy even though it cost half my tiffin allowance.

It wasn't long before I was in trouble with Popo again. After school finished each day we would go home in a rickshaw and during the journey the rickshaw-puller would unbutton his jacket. One hot afternoon Miew-kin and I were pulling faces at the strong smell of his sweat.

'Button your jacket!' I yelled to him. 'If you don't button it, I don't want to sit in your rickshaw.'

When we arrived at home, the rickshaw-puller complained to Popo about my behaviour and, once again, she beat me. Afterwards, just as she did every day, she welcomed Beng home from school, sat him on her lap and asked him what he had been doing. I watched as they smiled, laughed and talked in a babyish way to each other. I did not know what to think.

After school, we would do our homework on the veranda and then, in our free time, I would play with insects under the henna tree, or explore the *kampung* behind our house. My brothers and sisters stayed indoors. The boys liked playing in the bathroom, splashing each other and wetting the wall and floor. Miew-kin and I took care to keep away in case we were blamed for the wasted water. Our bathroom had a squat toilet at the far side and measured about seven by ten feet. In one corner, beneath the cold-water tap, an oval stoneware tub held more than a hundred gallons of water. Popo thought we would save money if the tap was left to drip continuously, day and night, so the water meter would run very slowly, if at all. Every day we each had a bath using an aluminium bowl to scoop the water and, by morning, the tub would be filled to the brim again.

One day some decorators were in the bathroom, re-painting the walls and ceilings white and touching up the black skirting. In the evening, when they left, they reminded Dai-chay to keep an eye on the wet paint. Dai-chay yelled a warning to us: 'Listen, all of you, the paint in the bathroom is still wet. You can use only the toilet. No one can bathe until tomorrow. Is that clear?'

Only my sisters and I responded, and I wondered what my brothers were up to. I found them sitting on the bath-room floor. Beng was trying to remove paint from his feet with a towel and I saw that the walls were smudged and streaked with black. 'Beng, you're in trouble now. Popo will surely punish you,' I cried, imagining her striking him with her cane for the first time. But he put down the towel and then, springing to his feet, he pushed me against the smudged wall. I lost my balance, turned to brace myself against the wall and, pressing my hands on the slippery wet paint, slid to the floor. Before I could get up, he shouted, 'Popo, come quickly! I saw her, Popo, she did it.'

My grandmother and my mother came running. I tried to tell them what had happened but they wouldn't listen to me. Popo flew into a rage and my mother held my hair in a tight grip to stop me running to the garden. Together they dragged me into the dining room and pushed me down by the teak table. My arms were pulled round one of the legs and my wrists were tied. Holding my left hand, Popo wove a chopstick between my fingers, then did the same with the right. She put my hands together and tied the chopsticks tightly at both ends, squeezing them against my finger joints. The loose ends of the string were tied round my wrists so that any movement would increase the pressure of the chopsticks against my fingers. There was no escape. The thin rattan cane, looped at one end for a handle, slashed down on to my back, delivering the first sting. 'Did you do it?' Popo screamed after each lash. 'Did you? Did you?' The more I cried out my innocence, the harder she beat me. As I struggled, the chopsticks tightened on my fingers and the string bit into my skin. Blood streamed from the cuts in my wrists.

Mother, believing that my brother would never lie, snatched the cane from Popo and rained blows all over me. 'Where did you learn to be so stubborn, Miew-yong? Is it from your father? Is it?' she asked, again and again. I tried to hold out against the pain, and take my mind to the places I enjoyed visiting in secret after I had delivered Popo's *chap-ji-kee* lottery stakes. I shut my eyes and pictured the giant trees in the botanical gardens with their huge exposed roots and imagined myself sitting on the low-hanging branch gazing at the water-lilies in the still pond beneath. After a while, Mother and Popo got tired of beating me and sat down to smoke cigarettes. They called the *muichai* to bring them tea. I thought they had given up, until Popo said I was to have nothing to eat or drink until I had admitted my guilt. I was left kneeling on the floor, tied to the table, while my family had dinner. Only Miew-kin felt sorry for me, but her fear of Mother was greater so she stayed silent. My father had not returned from his office and I suspected he had heard of my plight and stayed away. I knew he loved me, but he never had the courage to stand up to Mother and Popo.

After dinner, my mother and Popo returned their attention to me. I knelt on the floor resting against the table leg with my eyes tightly closed. Popo lit a grass wick, the same type she used for the oil lamp on the altar, and each time I protested my innocence she pressed it, lighted, to my lips to teach me not to lie. When tears ran down my cheeks, she doused the wick on my eyelids, to stop me crying. My lips and the skin round my eyes were soon swollen and blistered. 'If you want the punishment to stop, admit your fault and stop crying,' she shouted. In the end I gave in and said what she wanted me to say.

I did not cry again and I would not cry for many years. That night, I sleepwalked for the first time. I climbed on to a chair, unbolted the kitchen door, opened it and walked through our garden towards the Muslim cemetery, past the beautiful mauve bougainvillea, the orange bird-of-paradise and the huge cactus, which loomed dark against the night sky. Popo saw me go and watched me as I walked but she didn't wake me because she believed that the soul wandered during sleepwalking: should the sleepwalker be awakened, the *wan pak* might not return to the body and the sleepwalker would fall into a deeper sleep from which they would never return.

Many times, after that first night, my soul would wander while my bare feet took my body outside into the night and back again through the kitchen door, which I always bolted firmly behind me.

Nine

When a new black Wolseley arrived outside our house in January 1941 we were all excited. My grandmother and my mother had raised the money for the car by buying tontine shares, a method of investing that was popular with housewives. Few people had bank accounts and they had paid for the car in cash. That afternoon, when Popo went to the temple, she made Father drive her there in the car so that the people at the entrance would see her arrive in style. She boasted to her friends that she had paid for the car, and added that she had a clever way with money.

She ordered my father to drive her to the temple whenever she wanted to go there, but if he was annoyed by her manner, he did not reveal his feelings. He never made a fuss, and even when he was unwell he would take himself quietly to bed with a herbal brew until he had recovered. Only once do I remember seeing him lose his temper. He suffered from chronic piles, and whenever they erupted, Popo would heat live snails over a candle and drip their oil on to the piles to shrink the bleeding veins. After these treatments my father would sit on an old chair with a wide hole in the middle of the rattan weave. He had a similar chair in his office. One day, an itinerant weaver carrying coils of rattan over his shoulder walked by our house, calling his services. My mother ushered him inside to mend the broken chairs, without giving a thought to my father's predicament. At dinnertime when he realized what she had done, he took a knife and cut a hole in the centre of the new rattan on one of the chairs. It was unusual for him to act in this way but he was so annoyed that, for once, neither Mother nor Popo dared to upbraid him.

In August of that year, my little sister Miew-lan, who had been left with the *amah* since birth, began to cry constantly. Pregnant with her seventh child, my mother was always in a bad mood because of morning sickness. Not only was she unconcerned about Miew-lan, she would tell the *amah*, 'Take her to the garden and stop her making so much noise! Don't come in until she is quiet.' But Miew-lan did not stop crying and was banished to sleep in the servants' quarters. After weeks of crying, she looked tired and ill. Then the *amah* left suddenly, pleading a family bereavement. A few days later, Miew-lan became very distressed during bathtime. She was still small for her age and slow in learning to talk so she could not tell anyone what was wrong. That night my parents took her to hospital, where doctors found that she had serious fractures to her spine, which had occurred weeks or even months ago. They said that gangrene had set in and there was nothing they could do to save her.

We were not told that Miew-lan had died. After a few days, when she had not returned from the hospital, I approached Mother and asked, 'How is Miew-lan? When is she coming home?'

She slapped my mouth and warned, 'Don't you dare speak her name again in this house.' There was no funeral ceremony for Miew-lan, and we never knew where she was buried, and from that day she was called 'the number-six child who was lost'.

Not long after Miew-lan died, the air-raid drills began. Whenever we heard the sirens the five of us would grab our satchels and race to get under the teak table in the bedroom. As we sat in the darkness, protected by the kapok mattresses, I would think about the number-six child who had cried and cried, how she had gone to hospital but not returned, and how I must never speak her name again.

My father wanted to keep up with the war and spent a long time tuning our old wireless to the right station. Every evening, with Popo and Mother sitting nearby, he translated the news to them from English to Cantonese. Popo always interrupted with the same questions: 'Is the Japanese army coming near? Will Singapore fall?' and always he would reply, 'The British have big guns and many soldiers against the Japanese.' But once I overheard him telling a friend a different story. The Japanese army was pushing forward rapidly, he said. The soldiers were landing in Malaya from their staging point just beyond the Siamese border and this was possible because of an agreement between the Siamese government and Japan: if the Siamese helped Japan, they would not be harmed.

Soon even Father could not hide the news from us. The Japanese had captured Alor Star, to the north-west of Malaya, and Kota Bahru, capital of Kelantan, on the north-east coast. General Tomoyuki Yamashita, Japan's commander, later to be known as the 'Tiger of Malaya', ruled the air and sea after he had sunk four ships in the British Far East Fleet, among them the battleships *Repulse* and *Prince of Wales*, with the loss of hundreds of lives.

When I heard about the sinking I thought about Kung-kung, where he was and whether he was alive. I imagined all the dead sailors in the water with the fish nibbling their toes.

As we listened to the news on the wireless I began to wonder whether the Japanese would come to Singapore and become our new masters. I asked my father what he thought would happen. Father looked at me, and I could see that he did not want to frighten me but he said he believed that Singapore would come under siege. He confided that he could not share these thoughts with the family because he did not trust Popo to refrain from telling her friends of his views. He was a government servant, and they would think he had inside information. If rumours spread, he might be accused of scaremongering.

When the wealthy Chinese owner of the grocery shop near us decided to evacuate to Australia with his family, he offered his goods at below cost price to friends. My father knew this was an opportunity to stock up for a siege as the price of food was already shooting up. But the decision lay with Popo. We already had a large stock of salted dried fish, dried scallops, Chinese pork sausages and bacon in paper carrier-bags hanging from bamboo poles suspended from the kitchen ceiling, safe from the rats that ran about on the floor below. Father didn't know how to convince Popo to buy more without giving her the impression that we needed to hoard. He knew that if she realized how critical the situation was becoming, nothing would stop her telling her friends and causing panic.

After some thought he mentioned to her casually that the grocer was selling everything at giveaway prices, and named a few work friends who had bought from him.

Before he could suggest it would be a good idea for the family to stock up, Popo, not wanting to be outdone by other people, asked, 'Why did you not think of buying for the family?' She went to a locked drawer and brought out a roll of money. 'You'd better hurry before it's all gone,' she said. 'Buy whatever canned food they have, and some rice.'

By the time Father got to the shop the choice was limited and he had to take what was left. He bought cans of pork and beans, ham, cheese, condensed milk and soda biscuits. He bought six bags of rice, each weighing a hundred katties. The next day the grocer and his workers brought them all to our house on their bicycles and stacked them in the utility room, next to the kitchen, until they reached the ceiling. A padlock was fixed to the door and a tall cupboard positioned in front to hide it in case we were evacuated and had to leave the house unattended. Father said that it would be our gardener's job to move the cupboard and bring out the cases whenever anything was needed. When the food was safely stored Father, satisfied that we would not starve if the Japanese besieged Singapore, handed the key to Popo.

Popo and Mother had decided to give away the new baby for adoption, whether it was a boy or a girl. Popo, who was deeply superstitious and especially so since the death of Miew-lan, had consulted her astrologer on whether the animal sign for this seventh child could harmonize with those of the rest of the family. It was an important part of each person's identity. Many times Popo had told us how Buddha had called all the animals to sit round him to hear his wisdom, but only twelve had come; the rat was first, then the ox, the tiger, the rabbit, the dragon, the snake, the horse, the goat, the monkey, the rooster, the dog and the pig. Each year was dedicated to one animal, she explained, starting with the rat and ending with the pig, in a twelve-year cycle. People born in the year of a particular animal were endowed with certain qualities and characteristics and, by consulting the charts, compatibility among the signs could be determined.

'This seventh child will be born in the year of the snake,' Popo told us, and spoke of her dislike of reptiles, except as a delicacy. After the astrologer had studied the charts for my mother and her number-seven child, he had issued a grim warning: 'Your daughter is a tiger,' he said. 'The readings say that the life-water of this expectant grandchild will not be compatible with its mother's. This snake-child will cause three deaths in the family. It carries strong venom. It must not enter the family home.' He said that the new baby must be given away.

When we arrived at the hospital to see my newborn sister, I could see that my father was thinking about Miew-lan, and hoping that the new baby would heal some of the pain and that my mother would want to care for the child herself. I knew he was worried about employing another *amah* if my mother refused to look after her. When Mother told him about the astrologer's warning I looked at Father's face, but he turned away from me. He said we could not give the baby away, that these were foolish superstitions. Then he pleaded with Mother: it was sad enough to have lost one daughter, but to lose another was too painful to contemplate.

My mother turned on him. 'I hate caring for babies. If this one is not given away, I will engage an *amah* and she will suffer the same fate as the number-six child who was lost.' Father looked at her in disbelief. 'Everything has been arranged for the adoption,' she said. 'The baby will be taken away from the hospital as soon as the umbilical cord falls off.' My father put his face into his hands.

It wasn't long before my sister's fate was sealed. My mother's hairdresser, Mrs Ng, was also one of her closest friends. She and her husband were in their late thirties and had been married for many years but still had no children. They lived in a flat in Rochor Road, where the market stalls sold wild animals, and they ran the hairdressing business from their front room. Mrs Ng often complained to my mother, 'My husband wants to take a concubine because I cannot bear children. I would give anything to adopt a child from a good family.'

When Mrs Ng discovered that my mother was expecting her seventh child, she had appealed to my grandmother, not to my parents. She knew that my mother would do whatever Popo decided, and that my father would have no say in the matter. She also knew that Popo liked to be flattered. Calling her a 'good-hearted, merciful and kind friend', Mrs Ng begged for the child to save her marriage. 'Boy or girl, I will be eternally grateful,' she said, 'but I would prefer a daughter. She can help me with the hairdressing. I have prayed for a child for many years.' In return for the favour she promised to do my family's hair, 'free of charge, for as long as you wish'.

My new sister was five days old when Mr and Mrs Ng took her away from the hospital. They named her Kwai-chan and doted on her. However, filled with joy as she was to have a child, Mrs Ng spent all her time caring for Kwai-chan and neglected her husband. She knew he would not have minded so much if their adopted child had been a boy because he wanted a son to carry on the family name. To maintain harmony in the family, and because Mrs Ng was so taken up with Kwai-chan, she encouraged her husband to do what he had wanted to do before the adoption: 'Take a concubine. She can give you a son,' she said. So, when Kwai-chan was two, Mr Ng took a young concubine who was less than half his age. She was a virgin and quickly bore him a son.

Once a year, in mid-January, before the Chinese New Year, Miew-kin and I were made to go with Mother to Mrs Ng's place to have our hair permed. We never saw Kwai-chan while we were there and Mrs Ng would explain to Mother that she was at a birthday party or visiting friends, but I knew she was being kept away from us. My hair was always cut in the same way, aeroplane style, flat on the top with the sides flowing out, like wings, and then I would sit under the new electric perming machine with my wet hair rolled up in curlers. I was terrified of being electrocuted by the masses of metal hair grips hanging at the ends of a bunch of live electric wires. It didn't matter to my mother that I liked my hair straight.

Ten

Not long after my sister was given away, refugees poured into Singapore. Europeans arrived from Malaya by car and train; the streets were crammed with military vehicles and soldiers from Britain and the Commonwealth. The Raffles Hotel, about two miles away, was filled with Europeans and up on the hill, just a few minutes away from our house, the magnificent Goodwood Park Hotel on Scotts Road, with its wide entrance and ballroom that glittered with a thousand lights, teemed with the rich Europeans who liked to gather in its luxurious surroundings. Even with the threat of war and disaster, the Malay doorman stood on the red-carpeted stairs below the porch wearing his white uniform with gold epaulettes, gold buttons, and a black *songkok* on his head.

The senior British officers and their families lived in the best parts of the colony. Some officers, like our English neighbours, employed six or seven servants: a cook, a boy to serve, one or two *amah*s for the children, a laundry *amah* who doubled as a cleaner, a gardener and a driver. In running the colony the British favoured their own people and although, as an interpreter, my father was not in a race for promotion, he often saw non-white government workers passed over when they were better qualified than their white colleagues. Also, non-whites were not allowed to enjoy the lavish clubs or sports grounds and the better holiday bungalows near Changi beach that were set aside for government workers.

Under colonial rule the British controlled the broadcasting station and all government departments. The people knew little about the security plans for their island and could only try to guess what was going on by watching the behaviour of the Europeans. But most people, especially the Chinese, were only interested in making a living and, trusting in British protection, did not worry about the approaching Japanese.

As the war crept nearer, we heard on the wireless that British forces were retreating south from northern Malaya after bloody battles and that Japanese soldiers, with tanks and fighter planes, were about two hundred miles from Singapore. One morning it was announced that the capital of Malaya, Kuala Lumpur, was under Japanese control. Father believed it was only a matter of time before even more refugees would arrive in Singapore. The wireless said that after moving down the peninsula with surprising speed and defeating the British in Johor Baharu the unstoppable Japanese army was poised to deliver the final blow to the Lion City and capture the naval base in Singapore – the heart of British military power in the Far East. Singapore was supposed to be invincible and, with its cannons pointing south, facing the sea, prepared for the invaders. But the enemy had come overland from mainland Malaya in the north and only a narrow strait stood between them and our island.

I was at the Great World amusement park with my sisters and Sum-chay when the first bombs fell. Sum-chay often took us to the park to watch the Chinese opera because Popo and my mother did not enjoy taking us out:

they preferred to play *mah-jongg* with their friends. That day, before the opera, we went to one of the cafés where Miew-kin, Wang-lai and I had our favourite treat, ice-*kachang*, which was made of red beans and agar-agar, piled high with ice-shavings and streaked with the delicious multi-coloured syrup that always dripped down our chins. Sum-chay had her glass of *chendol*, coconut milk served with teardrop-shaped green bean flour noodles and *gula melaka*, brown sugar that came in tube-shaped blocks.

As we were leaving the café, the air-raid siren blared, but everyone in the park thought it was a drill and carried on as usual. Soon the lights from the stalls flickered out and people hurried to get off the rides. Children were screaming and everyone was running back and forth searching for the exits. Miew-kin, Wang-lai and I were crushed in the crowd, and held on tightly to each other. I could not see Sum-chay but heard her calling to us repeatedly, 'Run home quickly. Don't wait for me.' We ignored her and waited outside the gates, scanning the crowd and calling her name as men, women and children rushed by. We did not have to wait long before she found us. Then, frightened and shaking, we clasped each other's hands and ran home as fast as we could.

The wireless said the raid had killed more than fifty people and injured nearly two hundred. A bomb fell only two hundred yards away from our house but failed to explode. After that first raid the bombers came back again and again, and soon the air was filled with artillery fire and the scream of air-raid sirens, and the sky above Singapore hummed with Japanese planes circling the city. In the daytime the sky was dark with dense palls of oily smoke, which turned the raindrops black. At night it was bright with the flames from burning buildings. Those who had not already constructed air-raid shelters began to dig in their gardens to make something that would protect them from the bombs.

My father was a volunteer in the Civil Defence Force and worked tirelessly over the next two weeks to help rescue people from bombed buildings, and to remove the bodies of dead soldiers and civilians. He would return home and tell us about the fires that blazed everywhere, the streets littered with wrecked cars, the thousands of people who lay dead in the ruins, by the side of the road and in the monsoon drains. One day he heard that one of his closest friends had been killed in a direct hit on his shelter: he had been the first to jump into it and as soon as he was inside a bomb had crashed through the roof and killed him. His wife and five children, only seconds behind, escaped. After this we took up the red-haired devil's invitation to share his shelter. During the day, when the siren sounded, we ran across his garden and inside to safety. But when the warning came at night, we jumped from our beds and rushed under the teak table, remembering to snatch up our satchels packed with water and biscuits, as we had done many times during drills. At times we stayed there all night in the dark and fell asleep, except Popo, who would crawl out and grope her way to the altar in the next room, pick up her beads, kneel on one of the three cushions on the floor and chant her prayers.

The only light in the room where Popo prayed was the oil lamp on the altar and I could see it through the open door when I looked out from under the table. The flame danced on a single grass wick threaded through a metal ring held by three claws slotted on to the rim of a wine glass, filled with cooking oil and water. Above the altar glass-framed calligraphy, written in gold on bright red, extolled T'ien, the heavenly ruler. A white ceramic figurine of Kuan Yin, the Chinese goddess of mercy, and a statue of Buddha in the lotus position stood behind the oil lamp. On the altar there were offerings of scented flowers, small bananas, star fruit and mandarin oranges. The bowl for burning joss sticks was placed near the edge and in one corner was a brass incense-burner for sandalwood, which was used only on festive days. When I could not sleep, I would watch my grandmother kneeling in front of the altar, worrying at her beads, and listen to her muttered prayer for the bombs to stop.

When the bombing got worse, Father called the household together. 'There is great danger that our house could be bombed,' he said. 'We are so near the police station flying the Union flag. It will be safer for all of you in the countryside.' For once Popo agreed, and Father continued, 'I have a good friend who owns a chicken farm in Jurong, close to the south-west coast, and he will put you up. We will leave in the morning.' We went to pack some belongings, but Sum-chay and Dai-chay, our servants, chose not to come with us. They decided to return to their *coolie fong* to be with their fellow professionals.

The next morning, my parents, brothers, sisters, Popo, the two *muichai* and I, ten of us in all, crammed into the black Wolseley. My father would take us to the farm, then return to his duties in the city. As we drove there was a sudden downpour, and he had to peer through the windscreen as the wipers struggled against the rain. Eventually we turned into a narrow dirt track that cut through a coconut plantation leading to the coast. We passed beneath sixty-foot-tall coconut palms swaying violently in the wind and the car sent great sprays of muddy water on to the verges. I sat with my sisters on the laps of the adults in the back; we had a bumpy ride while our two brothers had the comfort of the front seat. Father tried his best to miss the pot-holes but every few minutes we hit a deep one and were bounced up, knocking our heads on the roof, then slamming down on to hard knees. The load was too heavy for a small car and Popo prayed that we would not get a puncture.

My father had met the chicken farmer at a police post in Jurong, he said. It covered a large country area and was run by Malays. On the way home from a fishing trip, his car had broken down. He had gone to the police for help and had met the farmer, who was trying to tell one of the policemen about a theft from his farm. The farmer spoke neither English nor Malay and could not make himself understood. Father said it was like watching a chicken trying to talk to a duck, so he asked if he could help. The farmer, speaking Fukien, explained that poachers had been stealing his chickens and entreated the policemen to patrol his farm. He said the thieves lived nearby and would be frightened by the sight of them. Father conveyed all this to the policemen, and the grateful farmer invited him to visit his farm next time he was passing, which he did many times.

As suddenly as the thunderstorm had begun, the sky cleared, and just before midday we arrived. The farmer waved a greeting and did not ask my father why he had brought his entire family with him. In fact, he seemed delighted to see us. He offered to put us up in his house and move his own family next door with his parents. I could see from my father's expression how touched he was and, satisfied that we would be taken care of, he returned to the city.

Once my father had left, my family went inside the house but I stayed outside to explore the farm. A short distance from the two farm bungalows there were several *attap* huts, which were used for storage and as sleeping quarters for the workers; they were partitioned and thatched with feathery palm leaves so they were cool and breezy, unlike the bungalows with their corrugated-iron roofs – they were like ovens in the hot afternoons. Chicken coops were raised high on stilts above the fish ponds, and I thought this odd until I spotted groupers darting up to feed on the chicken droppings. The farmer told us later that he sold the fish to restaurants, which served them sweet and sour; some of the fish were giants of nearly two feet long. Along the edges of the walkways between the ponds, female papaya trees grew, and although they were only about six feet tall their short, thick trunks were laden with fat fruit; close by, the taller male trees swayed in the wind, their tiny tasteless fruit, three or four inches long, hanging at the tips of drooping sinewy strands. The bombing sounded a long way from the farm and it was peaceful there. I looked up at the tall palm trees rustling in the breeze and laughed at the piglets following their huge mother, whose pink udders scraped the ground as she foraged in piles of smelly rubbish. As I watched the pigs tumble and play I forgot about the war until I was startled by a distant noise, louder than the rest. I remembered the Japanese silkworms and thought of my father in the city with bombs, wrecked cars and dead people.

Later that afternoon I needed to use the toilet and ran back to the house. One of the farmer's children led me to a small shed about twenty yards away, hidden from view. I approached it apprehensively as I had never used a bucket-toilet before. When I opened the door, the fetid smell hit me. The bucket was filled with excrement and buzzing with flies so I ran to some bushes in a quiet spot to relieve myself. The thought of the bucket put me off dinner that evening and I lied to Popo, saying I did not want any food because I had a stomach-ache. Had I told the truth, she would have accused me of insulting our hosts. I decided I would survive on the condensed milk and biscuits in my satchel.

That night, the farmer's wife, who was a plump, friendly woman and carried her baby on her back in a sling, showed us a box of mosquito coils and explained how to use them. She was concerned that, as city dwellers, we were not familiar with the hazards of burning them. She hinted politely at the precautions we should follow to avoid setting the house on fire. We burnt the repellent every night at home and knew of the dangers, but we did not want to appear ungrateful or rude so we let her explain. From under a table in the corner of the room she brought out the burner, a red metal plate about six inches in diameter with a rod in the centre. At the top of the rod a small flat ring held the coil. She opened the box, removed a coil and placed it on the ring where it unfurled. 'This is how you light it,' she said. She struck a match, tilted the coil and held the tip over the flame, immediately filling the room with the scent. 'Be careful. It's brittle and will snap easily.'

Miew-kin's legs were already red and swollen with bites and that night she reached for the burning coil to put by her bed. She had fair skin like my father's, and mosquitoes usually singled her out for her sweet blood. By dawn, once the repellent had burnt out, the mosquitoes were back in hordes and we were woken by their bites. My sisters and the *muichai*, Ah-pin and Yan-fok, both of whom slept in the room with us, were soon wide awake. We sat on our beds in the semi-darkness, slapping ourselves each time a mosquito bit. We took pride in boasting of the number of kills we made. Soon our arms and legs were covered with the bloody bodies of squashed mosquitoes.

At the farm we had no information about what was happening in the war. The farmer did not own a wireless because he couldn't afford to install electricity. Anyway, he had no interest in world politics. He said that, whoever ruled, farmers would still be needed to produce food. We waited patiently for news. Late on the afternoon of our third day, I saw my father driving up to the farm so fast that the black Wolseley was bouncing on the dirt track. He stopped the car, got out, rushed into the house and talked excitedly with Popo and Mother. Minutes later, all of us, including the farmer's family, were called together and told the bad news.

'There has been a lot of bombing in the city and casualties are high,' Father said. 'The Japanese have broken through the defence line in the north-west and thousands of their soldiers have crossed the strait from Malaya in boats and rafts and landed in Singapore. They will overrun the farm in a short time.' He had come to take us home. I was relieved to hear that we were leaving and ran to the bedroom. I collected my clothes, stuffed them into my satchel with the emergency rations of biscuits and water and waited impatiently to leave.

'Put your family into your lorry and come with us,' Father said to the farmer, and told him there were tens of thousands of soldiers from Britain and the colonies to defend the city.

'But how can I run?' the farmer asked. 'My father is

too old and my mother's bound feet will not take her far. Besides, everything I have is here, my home and my livelihood.'

The farmer reasoned that the Japanese army would need food and said he was willing to feed them in return for his safety and that of his elderly parents, and he told Father he would send his wife and children to a place to hide. My father tried once more to persuade him to leave but eventually he climbed into the car and drove us home, back along the palm-shaded dirt track, over the pot-holes, towards the bombs.

Eleven

We were driving slowly past demolished buildings, caught up in a heavy stream of cars and lorries as we made our way into the city. All the time our eyes scanned the sky, and it wasn't long before we saw planes coming out of the clouds, the rising sun on their wings. Mother and Popo, shivering with fear, broke into loud chanting. '*Om may toh fard. Om may toh fard*,' they kept saying, calling on Kuan Yin, hoping their incantations would protect us. My father said the planes might bomb at any minute and stopped the car. 'Quick! Run into the bushes and put your heads down,' he shouted. I grabbed my satchel, but Popo slapped my hand. We struggled out of the car and no sooner had we jumped into the bushes than explosions sounded a short distance away. We stayed hidden in the bushes until the planes had gone, then climbed back into the car and resumed our journey into the city.

As my father slowed down to turn into our drive I heard Popo and Mother gasp. Through the windows of the Wolseley I saw that bodies lay on the road blocking the entrance. Father reversed the car, drove across the road, and parked in the police-station compound. We climbed out and walked towards the house. All we could do was stare in horrified silence, too stunned to speak. Our concrete drive was a carpet of blood with bodies lying across each other, heaped in the monsoon drain and under the hibiscus hedges in our garden. Some lay in the foetal position and some faced down; others had stark terror in their open mouths and eyes. Most of the dead were British and Australian soldiers killed by machine-gun strafing from low-flying Japanese planes.

We tried to avoid stepping on the bodies as we made our way into the house. Wang-lai and Sai-ngau, the younger children, were glad to get out of the car after the long journey and seemed not to realize that the people lying on the ground were dead. They ran among the corpses trying to count them. Popo was furious when she noticed their antics. 'Such disrespect for the dead, you naughty girl!' she scolded, as she grabbed Wang-lai's hair and slapped her. Then she called my brother: 'Sai-ngau, come with me and don't be naughty like her.'

The front door was unlocked. 'Someone must have used a key to enter the house,' Mother said. Inside, our home had been ransacked. In the sitting room we had a rose-wood display cabinet with panels carved in a Chinese puzzle design, but the locked glass doors had been smashed and everything inside had been taken – the exquisitely carved jade miniature garden, the ivory dragon with its fireball, the antique porcelain plates and bowls Popo and her family had brought to Singapore from China.

Mother rushed to the altar and, to her relief, everything was in its place: the figurine of Kuan Yin, the statue of Buddha, the porcelain bowl for burning joss sticks, the incense burner, oil lamp and fruit offerings were covered in dust but untouched. She reached for the porcelain bowl, tipped the ashes on to a sheet of newspaper, and retrieved a parcel. She unwrapped it to reveal a small metal box, the size of a bar of butter. She opened it, and once she was satisfied that nothing was missing, she put the box into the inside pocket of her jacket. Then she refilled the porcelain bowl with ashes and put it back on the altar. From the drawer under the altar table she selected three joss sticks and a pair of red candles. She pushed the latter into the ash, one on each side of the bowl, lit them, then fixed the joss sticks in the centre and lit them too. Then she knelt down and thanked the gods for protecting her jewellery.

We ran into each bedroom in turn. Cupboard doors were flung wide open, drawers were pulled out and their contents scattered on the floor. The cheongsams in my mother's wardrobe had been thrown all over the room. The mattress was slashed where the thieves had looked for valuables hidden inside. The lipsticks and perfume bottles that had decorated my mother's dressing-table were gone. When she discovered this she cursed the thieves with all the swear words she could muster, then broke down and cried. Miew-kin and I made ourselves scarce lest she decided to vent her anger and misery on us.

My father went to the police station to ask when the bodies were to be collected. The removal of bodies from accidents and crime scenes was the responsibility of the police or undertakers they hired: ambulances would not transport the dead. When he arrived he saw that the police were stretched to their limit and it would be night-fall or the next morning before our drive could be cleared. In the confusion and disorder of the preceding weeks many unoccupied houses had been looted. Father decided it was futile to report the theft: there was little hope of recovering the stolen things.

When he returned from the station he found my

79

mother wailing about the bodies outside the house. She wanted to leave. 'I can feel the spirits of the dead,' she kept saying. 'The spirits are about us.'

My father tried reasoning with her: 'Where can we go? Who knows where the next bombs will drop?'

'I will not stay here while there are dead people lying outside!' Mother said.

He shook his head in exasperation. 'I don't know what to do. The police can't clear them away until tomorrow.'

Popo suggested that we should stay at Aunt Chiew-foong's place in Rangoon Road. 'Just until the bodies are taken away,' she said.

'What?' Father said. 'The children will get nothing to eat or drink there. They did not wash at the farm and need to bathe. What makes you think they will be allowed to use the water there?'

As always, Popo and Mother overruled him and it was decided that we should go to Aunt Chiew-foong's house.

'Go and bathe,' Father told us. Turning to Popo, he said, in a respectful manner because he did not want her to think it was a command, 'It would be wise to have a cooked meal before leaving and we should pack some food to take with us.'

'Cooked meal?' Popo said sharply. 'The servants are not here. Who is going to cook you a meal?'

'I'm not asking you to cook,' Father said. 'The girls can cook under your expert guidance.' He knew praise usually calmed her.

Luckily for us, the thieves had not taken the preserved pork, sausages, bacon and other dried foods that were suspended from the kitchen ceiling. They had not thought to look behind the big cupboard hiding the door to our storeroom either. As we walked into the kitchen, fragments of smashed crockery cracked and crunched under our wooden clogs. Popo was irritated by the noise so she told us to sweep the floor before we began cooking, and soon, sitting in a chair like an empress, she was giving orders. 'Yan-fok, cut down four pairs of *lapchong* and one half of a salted red fish. Soak them in cold water. Miew-kin, take a bowl and count out ten dried scallops. Soak them in cold water as well. And get two eggs. If you can't reach the egg basket, tell Yan-fok to get it. She's taller. Mind you don't break them. Ah-pin, pick up those clothes in the bedroom and wash them twice, then clean all the bedrooms. Wash away the thieves so I cannot see them.' I waited quietly for her instructions. 'Miew-yong, do you know how to light the stove?' Without waiting for a reply, she continued, 'Place a piece of *dama* in the centre of the stove. Better light two stoves. Arrange small pieces of charcoal next to it, then put a match to the *dama* and let it burn before adding larger pieces.'

Soon I had the charcoal burning steadily, then Popo told me to wash the rice until the water was clear. She dipped her middle finger into the pot to measure the amount of water. 'There, one notch. I don't like soggy rice.' She lifted the pot on to the stove.

We made a simple meal of rice with steamed pork sausages and salted fish, and a soup of eggs and dried scallops. It was my first hot meal in three days and it tasted delicious. After we had eaten, Father took us to Aunt Chiew-foong's house. He stayed in the Wolseley with us while Popo and Mother went up the few steps and knocked on the front door. No one answered. Planes droned in the distance and seemed to be coming closer, so Popo banged loudly on the door and called to my aunt. Eventually the door opened and my uncle appeared, my aunt beside him. He always had a stern face and hardly ever smiled, but now he was red with anger. He and my aunt must have guessed why we had come.

Before Popo could speak my aunt said curtly, 'What are you doing here? I cannot let you stay.'

'Only one night. Look, there is plenty of food for everyone,' Popo said. 'We can sleep on the floor and Poh-mun will not be here.'

'There is no room,' Aunt Chiew-foong said, and shut the door in her face.

My mother shouted and railed at the closed door, calling my aunt and uncle ungrateful. 'Have you forgotten what I've done for you? But for me you would have remained an old spinster.' Then she turned on my father. 'Couldn't you have said something?'

Father shook his head, got out of the car, and walked up to my mother and led her away from the door. He told her to calm down, and said to us, 'I'm taking you to my friend Mr Fu's flat but his home is always filled with friends. It might be crowded.'

Mr Fu and his family lived in the Tiong Bharu housing estate where the blocks of flats were lined up in rows. Father said that the Japanese had not bombed Mr Fu's street because it was so near the hospital. When we arrived, the Wolseley could not get to the block where Mr Fu lived because the roads were obstructed by bicycles, rickshaws, cars and lorries. Father decided to park near the main road in case we had to leave in a hurry. There were hundreds of people in the streets and Father explained that they had come from Java: they had thought Singapore would be able to stand up to the Japanese, and they were sitting all over the pavements, sheltering on stairways and sleeping on the grass verges or in monsoon

82

drains, cooking their food in square kerosene tins by the roadside. Outside Mr Fu's block some naked children squatted in an open drain and, beside them, a mother was holding a half-naked baby. The air stank of sewage.

We stepped over sleeping babies and young children and inched our way to Mr Fu's flat. When we got there we saw that the furniture was pushed against the walls, but even so there was little room for all the people inside. We squeezed in and found some space in one of the bed-rooms where babies were crying, children play-fighting and women talking about the bombing raids and their many friends who had been killed. Waiting to use the one toilet proved more than many could endure, and with each passing hour the room grew more fetid. The tiny space each person occupied was preciously guarded. Every time anyone left the room to use the toilet or to stretch their cramped legs, they forfeited their space. Each time I got up I had to stand by the door and wait until someone else moved so I could rush to take their place.

Father realized he had made a mistake in coming to Mr Fu's. With the Javanese refugees outside using the open drains as latrines, cholera and other diseases might break out. He wanted to take us home straight away. But by now it was night, the blackout restrictions were in force because Japanese planes were patrolling the sky, and he could not drive without headlights. We passed a sleepless night at Mr Fu's flat and left early the next morning before the others were up. At the bottom of the stairs and on the pavement, the Javanese refugees were still asleep. More had arrived overnight and it was difficult to get to the car. 'Be careful where you walk,' my father warned and, putting one foot cautiously after the other, we stepped over sleeping bodies until we finally reached the Wolseley. Driving back, we passed cars carrying Europeans going in the opposite direction, towards the wharves; foreigners were evacuating in earnest, but we could only return home and wait for the Japanese soldiers to arrive.

Four days later, on 15 February 1942, the Lion City fell to the Japanese. All the big guns that were supposed to protect our island never fired. General Yamashita had ordered the attack on Singapore earlier than planned because his army was short of ammunition. This decision turned out to be his greatest triumph. He had conquered Singapore several weeks in advance of the date set for the invasion by the Japanese Supreme Command and captured tens of thousands of rifles, machine-guns, field guns and millions of rounds of ammunition.

Father explained that General Arthur Percival's surrender of Singapore to General Yamashita was the greatest military defeat of the British Empire and that the domination of white men, who had ruled without challenge for more than a century, was now at an end. The greedy Japanese silkworms had ended their long journey across sea and land and had entered the city at last. Soldiers with bayonets fixed to their rifles patrolled every street, and in the streets near our house, we saw them round up many Chinese men and even boys. Only the Chinese were singled out; the Malays and Indians were left alone. According to Popo, this was because China and Japan had been sworn enemies since time began.

Father told us all to stay inside the house and we waited to see what would happen. One evening a Malay friend of his came to the door and I heard them talking in low voices on the veranda while I was reading a book in the bedroom. Father's friend was telling him about a ferocious battle that had taken place during the invasion at Pasir

Panjang Ridge. He said he had heard that the British and Malay soldiers had been bombarded by the Japanese artillery and were defeated, and described how he had gone to the *kampung* where his family lived to find out if they were safe. All he had seen were wrecked, abandoned buildings, and he realized that the people of the village had been evacuated before the battle had started. Inside their abandoned homes he found rifles, ammunition and uniforms strewn about the floor and said he believed the soldiers had changed into civilian clothes to make their escape. As he finished he lowered his voice to a whisper and told of how he had walked up to the ridge, to the scene of the battle, and seen bodies tied to the trees, hanging limply. 'Our soldiers had been brutally bayoneted over and over again,' he said.

Our house was about two hundred yards from the junction at the end of our road where a detention camp had been set up and prisoners were standing in the road guarded by Japanese soldiers. We watched as the number grew but, afraid that the Japanese would see us, we dared not open any windows or roll up the bamboo blinds. Instead we crowded at one end of the veranda where we could peep through the slats of the drawn blinds. Among the detainees there were boys as young as twelve. After standing in the hot sun for hours and after the guards had been changed, no one had been given water. They were not allowed to walk across the road to the latrines in the police station and had to relieve themselves in the nearby bushes.

That afternoon, as I watched the frightened people huddled in little groups, I spotted my father in the crowd. My heart leapt into my mouth and I called to my mother in alarm. He stood among a group of men surrounded by armed soldiers. I could see that the sight of those pleading for water distressed him, but although he spoke to the soldiers, it was clear he could do nothing to help. Some of the old and frail fainted and dropped to the ground, overcome by heat. Among the detainees I saw a few of Father's *mah-jongg* regulars. As I watched every movement, I told myself that the Japanese had no reason to kill my father or his friends.

Popo did not spare a thought for Father. She was concerned only for my older brother. 'Beng is as tall as those short bow-legged Japanese soldiers,' she said to Mother. 'What if they take him prisoner?'

She pulled him to the bedroom and whispered, 'Stay here and be quiet. If you hear knocking at the door, hide under the bed.'

'I don't want to stay in the bedroom. I want to see what happens to Papa,' he said, in the sing-song voice he used when he wanted to get his own way.

Then he broke from her grip and ran back to the veranda. Popo rushed after him and pulled him down on the settee next to her. She never hesitated to slap my sisters or me, but she had never hit or spoken sharply to my brothers. She always had a story to tell, and when my brother had quietened down, she began: 'At the time when the causeway between Johor Baharu and Singapore was being constructed, your grandfather gave your mother and me a fright.'

'What has the causeway to do with Kung-kung? Did he help to build it?' Beng asked.

Beng was always curious to know about our grandfather. As Kung-kung had had no son of his own he had treated my brother more like a son than a grandson. According to Chinese custom, daughters were not allowed to assume the role of chief mourner at a funeral, and could not perform the ritual for the dead, so Kung-kung was glad to have a grandson who could perform the ritual for him when the time came. This future obligation had been instilled in my brother when he was very young and he often wondered whether he would carry it out now that our grandfather had gone.

'One day, Kung-kung went for a haircut and did not return,' Popo continued. 'We worried for him because, at that time, there was a lot of talk in Chinatown of human heads being buried in the concrete to appease the spirits of huge structures built across water. If these spirits are unhappy, the bridges will collapse. We had heard that barbers were paid by head-hunters to put drugs into their customers' coffee. When they were drowsy, the head-hunters would take them away to cut off their heads. Many men went missing during that period. Fortunately, Kung-kung had not gone to the barber that day but had been out with his friends and was too drunk to come home.'

Beng's eyes were wide with horror.

'Last month,' Popo went on, 'the British army bombed the causeway as they retreated to stop the Japanese crossing from Johor Baharu. The Japanese are now rounding up people for their heads to repair the causeway.'

'Do you know how many heads are buried there?' he asked, terrified by Popo's gruesome tale.

'Oh, too many to count,' she answered. She always delighted in frightening her grandchildren. 'Now, do you want your head chopped off by the Japanese to be buried in the concrete?'

I watched through the bamboo blinds until the sun went down but my father had disappeared into the crowd and I did not see him again. That night I lay awake, alert to every noise, wondering what was happening to him. As I stared into the dark, I remembered Popo showing me the worm-like islands of Japan on the old, yellowed map and how far away the threat of war had seemed; I thought about the drills and the hours he and I had spent under the teak table as he told stories of the past; I pictured the peace and calm of the farm we had left and wished we had stayed there with the sow and her piglets. Since our return to the city and the bodies strewn across our drive, everything had changed. The war had become real to me and now I realized, with horror, that my father might be killed.

At dawn the next morning, I rushed to the veranda and looked out through the slats at the crowd of prisoners at the end of our road. Some were standing, others sitting or lying down on the road, but there was no sign of Father, and although I watched anxiously, I did not see him all day. That evening he came home looking tired and heavy-hearted, and slumped into a chair. The trauma of the relentless bombing of the past two weeks, with the uncertainty about the detention camp, had shaken him but, slowly, he recounted the events of the past two days. He told us that he had been detained on his way home and spent the night at the camp. That morning he had stepped forward when a soldier asked if anyone spoke Japanese and had been taken to the police station. He told us that when he arrived and entered the office previously occupied by his boss, the red-haired devil, he had almost passed out. A Japanese man in military uniform was sitting behind the desk and Father realized that the Japanese had taken over.

Clearly of high rank, judging by the veneration shown

to him by the soldiers, the Japanese officer spoke English with an American accent. After a long interview, my father was given back his old post as interpreter and instructed to start work immediately, translating for the soldiers who were questioning the people in custody. Before he left the office, Father plucked up courage to ask the officer if drinking water might be provided to the people in the detention camp. Then, escorted by a soldier, he went to the station store and found two pails, filled them with water, took a few cups from the canteen and carried them to the camp. When he got there, one man, driven mad by thirst, went berserk. He grabbed the pail and emptied the water over his face as he gulped it down. Another man yanked the pail away from him, but before a fight could develop, a soldier intervened with his bayonet. After they had watched my father make several trips to refill his pails, a few Malay policemen had fetched pails from their quarters and joined him.

Father told us that he had worked until late, interpreting the soldiers' questions in various Chinese dialects. After the detainees had been interrogated, many were released to return to their families. Some were put into military trucks and driven away. Father said he had watched their departure with foreboding. At that time, no one could guess the terrible destiny of those taken away. It wasn't until after the war that we discovered that many had been sent to work – and die – on the Siam–Burma death railway, and others had been executed.

'How can they be so harsh and prejudiced? We have the same skin colour, yet they want us to die,' Father said in despair. 'You must all be careful. My job doesn't mean we're safe. The Japanese government is not the same as the British and will execute the Chinese on suspicion.'

He leant back in his chair wearily. Looking directly at Popo, he said, 'You always call the Europeans "red-haired devils" and the Malays "Malay devils". If the Japanese hear you calling them devils, we will all be in trouble.'

Twelve

'All sorts of rumours are circulating in the temple. They say the Japanese devils are abducting young boys and shipping them to Japan to train for their army,' said Popo, one morning. No sooner had she spoken than there was a ferocious banging on the door. A group of Japanese soldiers with bayonets stood outside. Thinking they had come for Beng and Sai-ngau, Popo jumped up from her chair, rushed to where my brothers were sitting and pulled them into the servants' quarters, ready to escape to the back garden. As soon as they were out of sight my father opened the door and spoke with the soldiers in Japanese. I did not understand what was being said, but after they had talked to Father, they walked in and searched every room, gesticulating wildly. In the sitting room, one said something to another, then unplugged the wireless and took it outside. As they were leaving, they spoke to Father again. He reached into his pocket and handed them the keys to the Wolseley. We stood outside the door and watched as soldiers in dirty boots jumped into our beautiful car and drove it away. There was nothing we could do. After they had gone Father told us that some Japanese officers would be moving into the houses next door, vacated by British officers and their families. They would use our garage to store firewood.

Later that day, Mrs Chong, an old friend of the family, came to our house in great agitation. She had five children, all boys, ranging in age from ten to eighteen; she was the envy of mothers who had no sons. 'Kuan Yin favours her. Her star is bright,' the mothers would say, at the same time dismissing girl children. 'Daughters are rice barrels. We nurture them to serve others.' Mrs Chong's husband was a watch repairer who had a shop in Orchard Road, and the family lived in the flat above. He never overcharged his customers or lied to them about repair jobs so he prospered.

Popo ushered Mrs Chong inside and she sat down to pour out her story. Weeping and wringing her hands, she told us that her husband and sons had been taken away by the Japanese and for the past week she had been praying for their return. She told us that in the days before Singapore had fallen, she and her family had watched looters breaking into shops in their street and described how, armed with stout poles, her husband and sons had guarded theirs day and night. They had kept lookout from an upstairs window and threatened the looters with the poles. One night the looters had tried in vain to smash down the inch-thick wooden shutters to get at the watches inside. After the invasion they had kept the shop closed. Her husband and sons had not dared to venture outside because of the rumours that many male Chinese were being taken prisoner. They hid in the shop until one morning some Japanese soldiers, accompanied by the looters who had tried to break into the shop, banged on the door. When her husband opened it, the soldiers pushed their way in with the looters, who began to help themselves to the watches. When her husband protested, he was hit on the head with a rifle butt, and when her sons went to help him, they were beaten too.

'If we had known they would take such terrible revenge, we would have given them the watches,' Mrs Chong said, crying bitterly and clutching Popo's hand. 'The soldiers searched every room, and when they saw our wireless, one threw it on the floor and smashed it under his boot. Then they pointed their rifles at us and ordered us outside.'

Mrs Chong put her hands to her face, unable to speak as she struggled to contain her sobs. Then she told us how she had stood outside the shop with her husband and sons, who were bleeding from the blows to their heads, and listened to the glass showcases shattering, the furniture breaking. The looters had run off with as much as they could carry. 'A lifetime's work, all gone,' she wept. 'One soldier almost thrust his bayonet into my husband when he tried to sit down on the road. "*Kore! Kore!*" he said, in a harsh voice, and they made us all stand like this.' She straightened her back as if she was standing to attention.

As Mrs Chong spoke, my grandmother was sitting on the edge of her chair, leaning forward so she did not miss a word. I could see that her mind was already working on how she might turn the situation to her advantage. 'All this must have been very upsetting for Chai-chai,' Popo said.

'Yes,' said Mrs Chong, unhappily. 'My poor boy had a fit. He fell to the floor and started writhing, his mouth foaming.' Chai-chai, Mrs Chong's ten-year-old son, suffered from epileptic fits. Her astrologer attributed the ailment to 'the crazy goat' and predicted the fits would stop when he reached puberty.

She told Popo how her husband and older sons were powerless to help Chai-chai as he lay on the floor because they were beaten at every move they made. She, with a mother's instinct, had rushed to him, brushing aside the soldiers' warnings and reaching for the metal spoon she always kept in her pocket. As the soldiers shouted at her she pushed it between his teeth to stop him biting his tongue. After a few minutes the shaking had stopped and he lay still on the ground.

While Chai-chai was recovering, more soldiers emerged from the shop, laughing, chattering and admiring their new watches. Some had several strapped to their wrists as they climbed into their truck, taking with them her husband and four older boys, leaving her alone with Chai-chai. Mrs Chong had not seen them since and begged Popo to help her find them.

Always ready to make herself look important, Popo said promptly, 'Leave it to me. I will ask my son-in-law to make enquiries.' She turned to me and said, 'Miewyong, go quickly to your father's office and tell him to come home at once.'

I was shocked by what Popo had said to Mrs Chong, and as I crossed the road, I wondered how she could make such promises when Father had told us that the Chinese were being singled out for brutal treatment by the Japanese, and had warned us not to interfere in other people's affairs. I did not dare disobey her but I feared for my father. Would he still go out of his way to help others in trouble, I wondered, even if it endangered us all? Not wanting to disturb him, I loitered outside his office until lunchtime, then went in and gave him the message. He returned with me to the house, and after Popo had admonished him for taking so long, Mrs Chong related again the terrible incidents that had robbed her of her husband and sons. After every few words she broke down and cried, putting her hands together as if in prayer and begging

Father for help. Father looked at her anxiously but I could tell he didn't know what he could do for her, or what to say to comfort her.

'Plead with the Japanese officers,' Popo said. 'They must know where her husband and sons have been taken.'

Father's jaw dropped. Then he said, 'Are you mad? You want me to appeal to the Japanese officers? Don't you have any consideration for *my* life?'

For days Popo was furious with him. She liked to do favours for those of her friends, like Mrs Chong, who fawned on her, and her passion for flattery blinded her to the danger she had put us in. A few days later Father told her that he had asked some discreet questions about the whereabouts of Mrs Chong's husband and four sons but had been unable to find out anything and could do no more. 'There are spies and collaborators everywhere, seeking to gain favour with the Japanese. If they find out that I have been asking about prisoners it will amount to treason,' Father said, 'and the sentence is execution.'

He told Popo how only the week before a distraught mother had come to the police station weeping over the loss of her son and begging the Japanese soldiers for news of him. They had beaten her so badly she could no longer walk. All we could do was try to support Mrs Chong and Chai-chai, and hope that the war would soon end so that her husband and sons could return to her. When my mother visited Mrs Chong a few days later, she made it clear that she felt let down and no longer welcomed visits from us.

Popo had a wide circle of friends at the temple, and despite my father's refusal to help Mrs Chong, she still liked to boast about her well-connected son-in-law. On the first days of the new moon and the full moon, Miew-kin and I often went with her to the temple to hold her handbag while she prayed. Popo would buy joss sticks and candles from the temple shop and my sister and I would watch as she placed her fruit and flowers on the main altar with the other offerings. She would light a handful of joss sticks, raise her face to the sky and pray to the god of heaven, then place her joss sticks and pray again, first at the altar of Kuan Yin, then at the altars of the lesser gods. When she had burnt joss paper in the stone oven, she would give money to the temple, *shong yau*. A brass lamp with extended arms, each holding a wick in a saucer of oil, stood on the largest altar in the main hall. The caretaker would pour drops of oil into some of the saucers and announce the amount given by the worshipper. The loudness of his voice matched the size of the gift, and a large gift would attract the gaze of other worshippers.

When her prayers and *shong yau* were complete, Popo would kneel before her favourite god, Kuan Yin, to ask for favours and answers to her questions. She relied on a practice called *kao chim* to make up her mind on everything, big or small. She would vigorously shake a cylindrical pot which contained bamboo strips painted with different numbers until one fell out. Popo would place this strip in front of the figurine of the god, then ask if the number would provide her with a true answer by carrying out *ta-pui*: throwing in the air two crescent-shaped blocks of wood to see how they landed.

Ta-pui answered her in three possible ways. If both blocks faced upwards on landing, the answer would be wrong, so she would replace the numbered strip in the container and *kao chim* again. If they fell facing downwards, like overturned boats, that was unfavourable and no answer could be given, which would upset her. But if one fell facing upwards and the other downwards, the number would provide the right answer. In exchange for a small sum, she received at the temple shop a written interpretation printed on a small yellow leaflet that corresponded to the number on the strip.

After *kao chim* had answered her questions, we would follow Popo to another room in the temple where food was served at round tables to worshippers, free of charge. Each table seated ten or twelve adults and children, and at lunchtime everyone rushed for the seats. Popo's place was always reserved for her by her friends. It was no small honour to have a family member with a government job and she was respected for my father's position. After each visit to the temple, before she got into the rickshaw to go home, Popo would always make a show of throwing coins to the beggars who waited outside the gate. It was important to her that her generosity should be blessed by the gods and noticed by her friends.

Not long after Mrs Chong's visit, we were at the temple with Popo when a man she knew approached her and asked for her help in getting a permit for a shop. He gave her a bag containing two bottles of brandy and four tins of her favourite 555 cigarettes. That evening, after dinner, she mentioned the matter to Father and showed him the gifts. He was angry, but did not lose his temper. He took the brandy and the cigarettes, went outside and smashed the bottles on the ground; then he threw the cigarettes into the drain. When he came back, he spoke calmly to her: 'You know I have no power to grant permits, yet you accepted the gifts. I could lose my job and our home and be sent to prison.'

Popo seethed with resentment. Father's refusal to do

what she wanted would make her lose face; she was expected to give the man an answer the next week. In the days that followed she was distracted and I could tell she was working out what to do. I wondered if it had dawned on her that Father was less intimidated by her and that one day he might even ask her to leave. I thought about how her *chimui* would laugh if she returned to her home in Chinatown. They knew that Kung-kung had left her. If my father sent her away, her true nature would be revealed for the world to see. But Popo was artful and I knew she would not let this happen.

The day before she was expected to meet the man from the temple, she stood by one of the windows, watching for anyone coming up the drive. Every few minutes she went to the sitting room, put her head round the door to look at the clock on the wall, then went back to the window. I wondered why she was behaving so strangely and who she was expecting. I didn't think she could be waiting for Father, who always returned from work at this time, but I was wrong. The moment she saw him walking up the drive, she clutched her chest and crumpled to the floor at my feet, crying, 'I'm dying! I'm dying! My chest is hurting!'

The whole family, including Sum-chay and Dai-chay, rushed to her side. Mother knelt down and hugged her. 'Don't leave me! I won't let you die!' Beng, her favourite grandchild, held her hand and said comforting words to her, but Miew-kin and I watched the scene in disbelief.

The moment she heard Father's key at the front door, Popo gasped, 'Your husband is right! I will destroy this family if my friend even talks about the permit! It is better if I am dead. Why don't you ask him?' She beat her chest with clenched fists.

Father came into the room, looking perplexed at the commotion. Before he could ask, Mother rushed towards him and, without warning, grabbed his shirt, ripped it open, scratched his chest and face and spat at him. She had long, painted fingernails and he was soon streaked with blood. She went on beating him, but he did not raise a hand to her. Terrified by her fury, I wanted to pull her hands away from him, but I knew that she would only send me flying with a punch. Eventually, when the servants could not bear it any more, they pulled her off. Popo had put on a good performance and, for the rest of her life, she used the same trick to get her own way.

The next morning Father went to work covered with scratches and I followed him, a few steps behind. As he passed other workers, they shot him glances but no one was rude enough to say anything. When he went into his office I sat down outside. A few minutes later Mother arrived. She ignored me, flung open the door and went inside. She stood in front of Father, who was seated at his desk, and demanded to know what he was going to do about the permit. He repeated to her what he had said before, but she refused to listen. She went round the desk and started to hit him, shouting that he was a coward, until the men in the next room came in and dragged her away.

I could see that Father was embarrassed. Quietly he told them what the problem was. When he had finished someone told Mother to send Popo's friend to see him and he would try to sort it out. Father thanked him, went back into his office and shut the door. My mother walked down the steps and across the road without a backward glance. With burning eyes, I watched her until she disappeared. I knew I would never forgive or forget the torment and humiliation she had heaped upon my father.

Thirteen

As the Japanese tightened their grip on the island, many looters were arrested and punished. The cells at the police station were filled with prisoners, and stolen property was piled high in the storeroom next door. Father told us that it was an Aladdin's cave of silver candlesticks, trays, cutlery, Chinese porcelain plates and vases exquisitely decorated with blue dragons.

There were no more Europeans on the streets and western medicines were no longer available from pharmacies, but this did not affect us as my grandmother had always treated us with Chinese medicine. We could not buy imported goods in the shops, although they could be obtained on the black market at a price, but we had plenty of food left in our secret store. The condensed milk and soda biscuits helped to supplement our diet, but it had been a mistake to buy so much rice: the bags were crawling with inch-long worms. Miew-kin and I had to help pick them out every afternoon and feed them to the chickens in the back garden. Of course, my brothers did not have to perform this revolting task. In some of the batches of rice I scooped from the bags on to the tray, there seemed to be more worms than rice and I hated touching them. Each time I picked one up, it exuded slimy liquid and I had to run to wash my hands. Sometimes a worm would squirt me in the face when I pressed it too hard. Tired of my squeals and constant hand-washing, Dai-chay caught my hand. 'Here. Don't squeeze. Pick it up like this.' Holding a worm gently, she dropped it into a bowl of water. 'If you keep running back and forth to wash your hands, you will be here until sunrise.'

We became used to our Japanese neighbours and watched them as they relaxed in their garden in the evenings, sharpening their gleaming swords or practising martial arts. We had never seen a martial arts display before, let alone one performed by men wearing only a small pouch, and the first time we were dumbfounded.

Even Popo was open-mouthed with amazement. *'Ta kung fu,'* she muttered, her eyes on the soldiers, 'practised by monks in the mountains in China. But not like those Japanese devils, with no clothes on.'

'Do monks fight, Popo?' Beng asked, mimicking the soldiers with his fists clenched and one foot high in the air.

'Our monks have to protect the food they grow from thieves. Thieves like them.'

We were so engrossed that we did not hear Father come into the room. 'Get away from the window!' he said. 'The Japanese don't like people to watch. Do you want to annoy them?'

He shut the window overlooking their garden and told us never to open it when the soldiers were outside. But we still watched from other windows, catching glimpses of them between the trees.

The Japanese women were like their men: they were not in the least shy. While I was playing in our front garden I would see them dressed in elegant kimonos sitting in passing rickshaws. Sometimes they would call out to their rickshaw-pullers, prodding them with umbrellas to make them stop. Then they would get down, walk to the grass verge, lift their kimonos, squat and relieve themselves. They did not wear pants and were unconcerned about modesty, even with a rickshaw-puller looking on.

All the Japanese soldiers had close-cropped hair and I found it hard to tell one from another, which caused a problem. When our neighbours discovered that Popo was a herbalist, they asked her to prescribe remedies for their ailments. I had to deliver the medicines. 'Give it to that Japanese devil who came yesterday,' Popo would tell me. Often I handed the medicine to the wrong man and would have to endure unfriendly grunts and glares. I asked Father why the soldiers had such short hair, making them look so alike. 'Is it to prevent head lice?' I asked.

Father never brushed aside my questions, as Mother usually did: he always answered them truthfully. This time, though, he said he would only tell me if I promised not to repeat to anyone what he was about to say. 'It is not only for hygiene, but to cause the very problem you have with them,' he said. 'When they return to civilian life after the war, it will be almost impossible to identify those who committed atrocities.'

One day we heard a rumour that General Tomoyuki Yamashita was visiting the area. Father returned home to tell us there was a high security alert for his visit and we must take care to obey the order. It meant that roads would be closed to the public, all shops would be shut and the windows of every house had to be closed with the blinds drawn. We were warned not to look at the occupants of the cars flying the Japanese flag, and if we happened to see them on the streets, we were told to turn so that we had our backs to them.

After the Wolseley was taken away, my father had

bought a bicycle. He was the only interpreter in the office who spoke several Chinese dialects, and needed one as he was often sent out to record statements from crime victims. Sometimes he would take me with him, sitting on the crossbar. One day, he had to go to a plant nursery to take a statement from the owner concerning one of his workers who had committed suicide. He asked me to go with him and, although the crossbar was uncomfortable even with a cushion, I jumped at the chance. I treasured those excursions with Father. We would stop for snacks at coffee shops and roadside stalls, and he would let me push the bicycle up the hills. Also, safely out of Popo's hearing, he would talk to me about his childhood in China and laugh as he remembered happy days with his parents on their farm before the tree had fallen on his father and his mother had killed the monkey god.

During the journey to the nursery, we stopped at a roadside stall for cold drinks and, as we sat in the shade of a tree, I asked Father a question I had wanted to put to him for a long time but had not had the courage to do so. It concerned the yearly Ching Ming ceremony. Popo often sent me across the road to the Chinese cemetery to dig up the roots of the tall *lalang* for one of her remedies. There, I would watch people carrying out the traditional Ching Ming, the Bright and Clear Ceremony, which they did every spring on the graves of their ancestors. For six days in April, relatives gathered to clear the weeds and scrub the tombstones, make offerings of food, wine and joss sticks, and burn silver joss paper. When they had allowed enough time for the spirits to accept the food, they placed lighted cigarettes beside the wine cups for those ancestors who had been smokers. When the joss sticks burnt out, libations of wine were poured over the graves to signify that the ritual was over. Afterwards, the relatives would picnic by the graves, eating the food that had been offered in the prayers.

I knew that my father was a dutiful son who had loved his mother yet we never visited her grave during Ching Ming. Trying to choose my words carefully, mindful of being disrespectful or impolite, I said, 'Ching Ming is coming soon and people will be clearing the graves. Grandmother's must be covered with weeds. Why do we never visit her?'

He turned his head away and I thought he was not going to reply but as it would have been rude to ask again I stayed silent. But then he said, 'I did visit your grandmother's grave in the year that you were born, when I got my first job as an interpreter. I wanted to share the good news with her and let her know that she had her wish that I would not be a farmer, but I had to go secretly.' He explained that he could tell nobody of his visit to his mother's grave because if Popo had found out she would have been angry. Many years ago, when she had taken him in after Fat Lum had stolen his home, she had forced him to make a solemn promise that he would not honour his dead mother or ever speak her name. Father looked so unhappy when he said this that I knew I must never again speak of my grandmother's grave.

The time I spent with Father always passed too quickly, and soon we were at the nursery. As we walked between the lines of plants in search of the owner, I admired the beautiful orchids. I hadn't known there were so many different varieties and I struggled not to touch them as my father told me their names. Dendrobiums, with their long stems of delicate flowers bending downwards, grew in hanging wire pots filled with charcoal and broken brick.

The potted vandas, with up to sixteen flowers and buds on a single stem, were on raised wooden stands in blazing sunlight. Spider orchids, grown for the cut flowers, were planted in the ground, like hedges. As I looked at them I imagined the garden I might have when I was older.

We found the owner and, speaking in Teochew, he told Father what had happened. Over the past few weeks many of his orchid seedlings had withered and he had warned the man who worked for him to be careful when he was handling them. One morning, he had found a whole section in the greenhouse dead, and when he examined them he discovered that concentrated pesticide had been poured over them. He showed my father a rattan basket holding coils of tuber roots: steeped in water for a week, they produced a toxic solution that he used to control pests. He told Father that he suspected the seedlings had been destroyed by the man's carelessness and he had threatened to report him to the police. Two days later he had found the man's body in the bushes, with an empty cup that smelt strongly of pesticide beside it.

When we left the nursery, and I was perched on his crossbar, Father explained how frightened the man would have been at the threat to report him to the police: people were often beaten first and questioned later. He explained that the poison must have caused a slow, painful death, yet the nursery owner seemed to care little about what had happened.

As Father pedalled home I thought about the man who had worked among the rows of dendrobiums, vandas and spider orchids, of how he had been careless and killed the seedlings, and had ended his life in the bushes by drinking poison.

Fourteen

The next day, while we were having breakfast, my father told us that he had hired a tutor for Beng, Miew-kin and me, as we were the eldest, and we were to have Mandarin lessons three times a week, starting the following morning. I had not had a lesson since the Japanese closed my English school, and had enjoyed spending my days idling outside.

When I met our tutor for the first time she gave me an austere look from behind small round black-rimmed glasses. Tall, slim and around thirty, she wore a calf-length printed-cotton cheongsam and from her leather bag she handed out writing brushes, sticks of black ink and four-inch-square stone slabs. We began our first lesson by learning to write with the brushes. When we needed more ink, we would put a few drops of water on the stone slab and grate the ink stick into the little puddle: we made ink as it had been made for centuries. The stick was the soot of special hard woods, like olive or grape vine, mixed with gum arabic and rolled into shape. We had our lessons at one of the square *mah-jongg* tables in a corner of the veranda. The doors to the sitting room and our bedrooms were left open during the day for fresh air and light, which meant we were often distracted by what was going on in the house. Our teacher was annoyed that we could not have a room for her lessons, but she was too polite to complain.

Except for my parents' bedroom, there was no privacy in our house and all the keys to the internal doors had been removed. There was a spare room, but Popo insisted that my brothers, sisters and I slept in hers. 'Why do we have to crowd into one room when there is a spare one?' I often asked her. We children wanted a room of our own, especially when we were not sleepy and wanted to turn on the light to look at the Chinese comic books Mother rented from the grocery shop for my brothers. Instead, we would sometimes stare into the dark all night until we heard the cock crow.

'I want to observe how you sleep,' Popo said. 'It can tell me whether your future will be good or bad. Wang-lai sleeps on her front, like a frog. That is why I keep her on my bed, to cure her of the habit. She's had enough smacks not to sleep in such a crawling manner.'

My brothers shared a double bed, as did Wang-lai and Popo, and there was a single bed for Miew-kin and me. Miew-kin's snoring was so loud that I usually slept under the bed with cotton wool in my ears. Every night before bedtime, we had to parade before Popo in our pyjamas for the hygiene inspection. After she had examined our hands and fingernails, we were made to sit down and lift our feet one at a time. If she saw any dirt, we had to wash it off before we got into bed. Then she would tell us a story: we had to sit up and listen until she reached the end even if we were sleepy. She only told scary tales about disobedient children. One in particular, which I knew by heart, was about a man-like monster who lived near her village in China. Its body was covered with long hair and it fed on the flesh of children. One day the monster went down to the village disguised as a sweet-seller and met a greedy, disobedient little girl who had spent all her money on sweets but wanted more. The 'sweet-seller' invited her to go with him to his home in the mountain and told her it was filled with sweet things, and that she could eat to her heart's content. She went with him to the mountain and did not return that night.

The next day, the 'sweet-seller' was back in the village. The little girl had an older sister who had been searching for her. Knowing that her little sister was very fond of sweets, she asked the disguised monster if it had seen her, then described her clothes and the gold ring on her sister's little finger. It said cunningly that it had seen a small girl of that description near its home on the mountain and offered to take her there. When they arrived, it crept up behind the older sister, caught hold of her and put her into a cage where she watched as it removed its mask and clothes. Then it gave a loud roar, sat down and ate a huge meal. Afterwards it belched loudly and began to pick its teeth. Trembling with fear, the girl caught sight of something gleaming on the toothpick it was holding: her little sister's finger with the gold ring. Popo always ended this story with a warning: 'If you are greedy or disobedient, the monster will come and eat you.' Her bedtime stories frightened me. On many nights I did not dare get up to go to the toilet so I sometimes wet the bed. When this happened I dreaded morning when I would have to face a scolding from Mother and laughter from my brothers and the servants.

I was in bed one evening, recovering from stomach-ache. The day before, I had climbed the cherry tree and found that the ripe fruit was full of holes with ants crawling inside and eaten the half-ripe ones, which had made me ill. As I drowsed, I heard Popo and my parents enter the room and shut the door behind them. Assuming I was asleep, Father stood on a chair by the wardrobe, reached up and pushed open a panel to reveal a secret compartment with a small wireless inside. He placed it on the table by the wardrobe. Keeping the volume low, he tuned in to the English news and began to translate it to Popo and Mother in Cantonese. Then he climbed on to the chair and put the wireless back in its secret compartment. As I watched him hide it I knew, without being told, that I must never talk about it.

Once it was safely concealed once more, they began to talk softly. Father was saying, 'The Japanese officer had a chat with me today. When he learnt that I had five children, he asked, "How many are studying Malay?" I had to lie and tell him that one child is at school, two are sickly and two are under six.' Normally calm, he sounded anxious and there was fear in his voice. His next words made Popo jump. 'Beng must enrol at the Malay school tomorrow.'

'You must be mad, sending your eldest son to study that language,' she snapped. Beng was the apple of her eye and she could not imagine him mixing with 'devil children'. In a raised voice − not caring if she woke me or not − she continued to berate my father: 'And if you're thinking of sending Miew-kin, you can forget it. Her prayers for atonement cannot be interrupted.'

Miew-kin's sins were cited in the *Book of Three Lifetimes*, a type of household almanac based on the time and date of birth that reveals the virtues and transgressions of the past life. It offers advice on the kind of penance to be carried out in the present lifetime to obtain deliverance in the next. According to Popo's interpretation, Miew-kin had been a man in her previous existence. She had lived the life of a rogue and violated numerous virgins.

'The flower debt must be repaid during this present life,' Popo had told the family. 'If not, she is doomed to be a whore, not only in this life but in the next as well.'

When Miew-kin had reached seven, the age at which Popo believed a child could understand the importance of atonement, Popo had instilled in her the need to repay the flower debt. She was so convinced and frightened that she submitted meekly to Popo's wishes. During our afternoon playtime we were given newspapers and scissors and would spend hours cutting out shapes of people, but Miew-kin was not allowed to join in. She had to kneel in front of the altar doing penance. With a string of one hundred and eight prayer beads round her neck, and a bowl of scented flower petals placed on the altar in front of Kuan Yin, she would kneel and chant, '*Om may toh fard*,' once for each bead, to save her in rebirth and to beg pardon for the sins of her past life. There were times when, half-way through, she would fall asleep and crumple to the floor. When this happened, I would shake her, waking her before Popo noticed. She would sit up, stare blankly ahead for a moment, then continue her chanting. As well as her daily prayers, Miew-kin had to perform other acts of atonement on the days of the new moon, the full moon and the festivals of the gods. On those days, she held a lighted joss stick in one hand and a sheet of yellow paper printed with small red circles in the other. Reciting the same mantra, she would pierce the centre of each red circle on the paper. It took her more than an hour to complete the burnt offering. Popo made sure that she never cut short her penance, but the endless prayers, chants and offerings slowly killed my sister's gentle spirit.

Since Popo would not allow her eldest grandson, Beng, to attend the Malay school, Miew-kin's prayers for penance could not be interrupted and I was too ill to get out of bed, Father suggested that Wang-lai should go to the Malay school. 'She is just the right age to start her education,' he said, and thought the matter was settled.

'Wang-lai?' Mother asked incredulously. 'She has never been out alone and cannot speak a word of Malay.' Then, pointing at me, she said, 'Miew-yong mixes with the Malay girls from the *kampung*. She should go.'

Father looked at me, lying in bed with my knees up to my stomach, and objected: 'Miew-yong is still recovering. She's not well enough to start school tomorrow.'

'I'll see that she's well by morning. A potion tonight will clear her stomach.'

I flinched when I heard what Mother had in store for me. That night I had the *mungsa* treatment again, and this time my mother insisted on doing it. When Popo performed the *mungsa* it was bad enough but Mother was stronger: she always took care of her health and regularly ate Boh food and drank fine wine. 'Food is medicine and medicine is food,' she would say, and for our evening meals the servant would mix herbs with steamed bird's-nest soup, or steamed winter melon and chicken, or lotus roots and pork boiled for many hours.

Mother's strength combined with her temper would make her *mungsa* treatment a terrifying ordeal. I also knew that if I uttered so much as a whimper she would not hesitate to slap my face, no matter how ill I was. I braced myself to hold out, even when the pinching reached my armpits so I would not make things worse for myself. As she began to pinch me I ignored the pain, closed my eyes tight and went to the still place in my mind where I could see the pond, myself resting on a bough and reaching down to touch the white water-lilies floating on the water beneath.

That night Popo's cure-all brew made me so sick that I felt as if all my insides were pouring out. Eventually I fell asleep but woke just after midnight feeling hungry. I knew that in the morning I would be allowed to eat four soda biscuits, two three-inch-long bananas and drink a cup of sweetened condensed milk, and that I would have this meal three times a day for seven days, regardless of how quickly I recovered. 'Clear the poison with bitter herbal brew and keep the stomach empty,' was Popo's answer to all ailments. The thought of enduring that meagre diet made me feel even hungrier until I could wait no longer.

Dai-chay's kitchen was out of bounds to children and she would shoo us away as she drove out the chickens when they strayed inside, by swinging her plump arms. I thought about creeping into the kitchen for some food but it was too risky: the door was shut at night to prevent the *muichai* stealing, and the latch made a loud, grating noise when it was drawn back. I knew that if I tried to open the door I would wake the servants, but I was too hungry to sleep or even to worry about having to start at a new school in the morning. Instead I kept thinking of the fruit offerings glowing in the darkness upon the altar in the dining room. I feared the anger of the gods if I stole their fruit but I couldn't put the idea out of my mind. In the end my stomach rumbled so loudly that I got up and crept to the altar, knelt down and kowtowed many times to Kuan Yin. Then I asked her permission to eat the star fruit and a bunch of succulent bananas. I picked up the star fruit but replaced it when I realized

I had no means of slicing it. Taking care not to knock over the burning oil lamp, I took several golden bananas instead, then crawled under the altar table, ate them quickly and hid the skins behind the potted palm in the hall, reminding myself to throw them away first thing in the morning when no one was about before the servants had cleaned the house.

Early next morning I collected the banana skins and, as the dustbin was in the kitchen, threw them into the deep drain by the drive. I waited to see if Popo would notice that they were missing from the altar when she went to say her morning prayers, but I was not afraid as no one had seen me take them. I believed that only the gods knew what I had done.

In the bedroom, Ah-pin was combing Popo's long hair, which had never been cut, into a neat bun at the back of her head; she had never done her own hair, and before she had bought Ah-pin, my mother had arranged it each morning. I watched and waited until finally Ah-pin pushed the jewelled hairpin, a square jade surrounded by twelve natural pearls, into the right side of the bun. My eyes followed Popo warily as she moved towards the altar. Holding the bundle of joss sticks to the burning oil lamp, she gave a shout of astonishment. 'The gods have feasted on my offerings,' she cried in delight. 'Look! The bananas have been blessed.' Her excitement brought my mother and the servants running to the altar, and I hid a smile behind my hand as they fell to their knees and joined Popo in lighting joss sticks. For the whole week that sacred event was the main topic of conversation.

Popo never did find out what I had done and she never became suspicious that, whenever I was ill and on a diet, the gods came to feast on the fruit offerings. I shared the secret with Miew-kin and the *muichai*, and when nobody was around we would giggle about Popo and the bananas blessed by the gods. I never told Beng and Sai-ngau or Wang-lai: she was Mother's eyes and ears, and I knew she would not hesitate to betray me.

Fifteen

I rode on the crossbar of my father's bicycle to my first day at the Malay girls' school off Tanglin Road. I was wearing the uniform of the English school I had attended before the war, which, luckily, matched the colours of the white *baju* and blue sarong the Malay girls wore. Father and I went to the office of the headmistress to register. She was a middle-aged lady wearing a pink *baju* and matching sarong with a light blue *tudung* over her shoulders, her hair in a bun at the nape of her neck. Father told her that I was eight and that I spoke Malay, and asked if I could join a class of pupils my age instead of the beginners' class. He explained that, as a linguist, he had helped me to catch up with reading and writing in Malay and Arabic. As he spoke, I realized he wanted to save me the embarrassment of being the oldest girl in my class. The headmistress understood this too and set his mind at rest, telling him that there was no shame in older children from other races joining the beginners' class.

I soon settled in. We did not spend all our time in the classroom: we also went on nature-study trips to the botanical gardens, where I would often come to sit by my special water-lily pond when I fled from the noise and arguments at home. There, we sat in small groups with paper and pencil in hand, looking up at the trees, noting the different birds we could see and watching the monkeys swinging from branch to branch or feeding on the wild palm nuts and fruits. We were forbidden to follow them into the woodland because they were adept at snatching food from careless hands and pulling hair.

After a few weeks at school I made friends with some children from another class who were the same age as me. They lived in the Malay *kampung* and we often walked home together. My short-cut led me through the noisy *kampung*, which smelt deliciously of simmering curry and *sambal*. The long, single-storey wooden buildings in the *kampung* were partitioned into one-room dwellings and each was topped by a corrugated-zinc roof that stuck out a few feet beyond the front entrance to provide shelter from the rain on a long, narrow veranda. A low bench stood at the entrance to each dwelling with a wood-burning stove on it and a set of saucepans. The veranda was a kitchen as well as a gathering-place for women and children, and in the hot afternoons, the women sat talking on the floor with their naked children playing at their feet. As they gossiped they would let down their hair and expertly crush lice between their thumbnails, then slick coconut oil through their tresses and deftly twist them back into a glossy bun.

The Malays had large families, and many women in the *kampung* had given birth to nine or ten children by the age of thirty. Whether they were boys or girls, they were treated the same and loved by their parents and grandparents. The Malays never gave away their daughters and I wished that my family thought the same way. The young married women in the *kampung* were often pregnant and I would sometimes see a woman with one baby bulging in her stomach and another wrapped in a sarong on her hip, doing her chores or walking with a basket of shopping balanced on her head.

Between the *kampung* and our house there was a playing-field, separated from the bottom of our garden by a hibiscus hedge. It was a meeting-place for the Malay families and I went there to play rounders or to take part in celebrations like wedding feasts, children's parties, funeral vigils and circumcision ceremonies. The preparations for a wedding feast could last for several days, with everyone chipping in to help with the cooking and decorations under a huge tarpaulin that protected them from sudden downpours. Women sat on grass mats cutting up baskets of vegetables, peeling shallots, garlic and ginger, slicing lemon grass, grating coconut and grinding fresh spices on large stone slabs with granite rolling pins, while the men butchered animals, cutting up goat and chicken for curry.

Whenever I was invited to a wedding, I would bring bunches of henna from the tree in our garden and help the women slice sweet-scented *pandan* leaves into hair-thin strands to mix with the champaca, rose and jasmine petals that were piled high on trays and placed at the foot of a dais for guests to help themselves to as a memento of the wedding. The dais was covered with layers of sumptuous sarong fabric and cushions, and this was where, when the ceremony began, the bride, her hands stained with henna, sat beside her groom to welcome the guests. Nearby a dance-floor, made of wooden boards arranged by the young men on the uneven ground, was lit with coloured lights fixed to posts. After the wedding ceremony and the feast, the celebrations would continue late into the evening with a band of musicians playing drums and accordions for the *ronggeng*, a popular Malay dance. The

117

men wore Malay costume and the *songkok*, and the women, in colourful sarong *kebaya* and *tudungs* over their shoulders, decorated their hair with flowers and wore lots of makeup. They would dance a couple of paces apart, moving in tiny steps to the rhythm of the music, and inviting the audience to join in. Soon everyone would be dancing.

Fatimah was my best friend. She was the second of nine children and the fairest girl in the Malay *kampung*. Her long black hair was parted in the centre and held back with two green butterfly clips and she had big brown eyes, twice as large as mine. I first noticed her at one of our school outings to the botanical gardens. We were all sitting by the lily-pond with pencils and paper, drawing the fish and tadpoles that patrolled the murky water beneath the white, cup-shaped lilies when she dropped her pencil into the water. Without a word she lifted her sarong, stepped into the pond, and retrieved it before the teacher noticed. She was a perfect friend because she loved to explore as much as I did. After school she would rush home and change out of her *baju* and sarong into a short dress. As she was the eldest daughter she had to do some chores and care for the younger ones while her mother did the family's laundry, but in the late afternoon I would join her and a few other friends to have fun.

Once we took a short-cut to Orchard Road through a field of sugar-cane on Anguilla Park and the Chinese owners pelted us with stones. A week later we paid them back by pulling out their sugar-cane. We had prepared our escape route in advance and made sure the family was outside to see the tops of the sugar-cane shoot up in the air as we pulled them out. We soon heard screams, shouts and running footsteps but we were faster and by the time they caught up we were in my Japanese neighbours' garden, looking innocent. The Chinese family stood outside and did not dare set foot in it. Another time, we went out when the twelve-foot-wide monsoon drain along Orchard Road was swollen with fast-flowing water after hours of rain and played chicken, walking along a four-inch-wide cement arch across the drain. I was sad when Ramadan came and Fatimah could not come out to play because she had to fast from sunrise to sunset in the holy month. Afterwards, she told me how difficult it was not to eat or drink, and that she was not even allowed to swallow her saliva and would have to spit endlessly.

Fatimah's home was a long room with a raised platform in one corner. It was a bed for her parents and the younger children, while the older ones slept underneath. A curtain was drawn to hide the sleeping area in the daytime, and there were cushions on the floor instead of chairs. The first time I visited, I saw a child sleeping in a sarong that hung from a spring in the centre of the room. As I looked at Fatimah's tiny sister, sleeping in the swaying sarong, I remembered my own little sister, the number-six child who was lost, and I thought how she might have lived if our *amah* had been allowed to use one of these as she had asked. 'Sometimes I fall asleep carrying her,' she had complained to my mother, 'and my arms are so tired that the child may slip to the floor.' But Mother and Popo would not hear of it. 'This is not a Malay house,' they had said.

Fatimah's parents were gentle and kind. One day her mother was getting lunch ready and I was sitting with Fatimah, her father, brothers and sisters as they waited for the meal. A clean white cloth was spread over the mat and a pot of tapioca, a plate of fried anchovies and a bowl of hot spicy *rojak*, with pineapple, cucumber and the tops of tapioca plants, was laid out on it. Some of the neighbours' children were standing in the doorway, staring hungrily at the food. I felt it was the right moment to leave so I uncrossed my legs to stand up, but Fatimah's mother held out her hands and gestured to me to stay. '*Jangan pergi. Duduk, makan*,' she said, but I shook my head politely as I could see that there was barely enough food for her family. Then looking hurt, she said, 'You don't want our food because you have plenty at home.' I realized that, without meaning to, I had insulted her. I mumbled an apology, sat down again and ate as sparingly as I could.

Afterwards Fatimah's father took out his betel-nut holder, spread some lime on a leaf of betel pepper, added a small slice of the nut and a little cardamom, then folded it into a small triangular bundle. I had always been curious about why people chewed betel and what it tasted like. He noticed my interest and smiled at me, revealing reddish-stained teeth. Then he handed me the little parcel and told me to chew it slowly and not to swallow my saliva but to spit it out. When I tasted it, I screwed up my face, spat everything on to the floor and everyone laughed.

At home my father made sure we continued reading and writing English so that we would not forget what we had learnt, and he spoke to us in English whenever he could. Every Sunday morning he gave English lessons to Beng, Miew-kin and me, and afterwards he would take my sister and me to a Chinese restaurant in Orchard Road. The restaurant was among a row of shops opposite Singapore Cold Storage, and on the way Miew-Kin and I would press our noses to the window of the toy shop, gazing at the dolls Father did not dare buy for us because Mother said they were a waste of money.

Doh Wu, the restaurant, was clean and bright with

grass green tiles on the walls, flowers in ceramic vases hooked to the walls and many potted palms on the floor. Father always chose a side table and ordered fried prawns with cashew nuts, steamed glutinous rice with chicken and stir-fried ho fun noodles with prawns and bean-sprouts. Afterwards we had sweet almond egg custard.

Now that I was at school again, I did not have lessons at home with my brother and sister, but when they did their homework in the afternoon, I had to sit with them, copying what they had been taught. Writing the characters with the Chinese brushes left my fingers stained with black ink. 'I am already learning Malay and striving to catch up with that,' I explained to Popo, trying to make her understand that I couldn't manage Chinese as well, but she was deaf to my protests. One afternoon, during a heavy thunderstorm, when I was painstakingly copying characters, I heard Fatimah and some other girls from the *kampung* calling to me. I could see they were carrying baskets and running about in the pouring rain. Earlier that day, the sky had looked threatening and they had told me that, if there was a storm, I could help them collect mangoes blown down by the wind.

I went to the window and signalled to them to wait for me, but I could not invite them in – Popo never allowed my Malay friends into the house. 'They are not coming in here because they have lice in their hair,' she had warned the servants. They waited outside while I had my eyes fixed on the clock, willing the hands to move. At last the study session was over and I rushed to the storeroom, grabbed a basket and ran out of the house to join them. Behind me I heard Popo yelling, 'The rain is too heavy. Come back!' I ignored her. I knew I would have to face the consequences later, but as hardly a day went by without her beating or scolding Miew-kin and me, this disobedience could not make things worse. Anyway, I wanted to go out in the storm with my friends.

We were soon soaked, but we loved playing in the warm rain, heedless of the thunder, the lightning flashes and the fierce wind. Outside, I could forget the fear and unhappiness I felt at home. We ran past the Muslim cemetery beside my house, through the *lalang*, oblivious to the sharp edges of the long grass, then picked our way through the thick undergrowth of bamboo and thorns until we entered a clearing. Hundreds of green mangoes covered the ground and as I gazed at them the wind caught the branches and shook off more, with several green and brown chameleons that scampered across the fruit and into the bushes. We filled our baskets until they were too heavy to lift and had to drag them home. I could not remember Dai-chay buying unripe mangoes, as these were, and I asked Fatimah what her family did with them. She said her mother gave some to their neighbours and made the rest into a hot pickle.

When I got home, Popo was resting with her feet up. It wasn't long before the evening's *mah-jongg* session so I was hoping to get away with a dressing-down and no dinner. I approached her warily and gave her the basket of fruit, hoping she would like the idea that Dai-chay could turn them into pickle.

'You'll catch cold,' she said, watching the water drip from my wet clothes on to the floor. 'You know quite well that we don't eat unripe mangoes. Put them into the dustbin. You will not go out again with the Malay girls.'

Sixteen

By the end of 1942, food was in short supply. Many of those who had believed that the Lion City could not fall to the Japanese silkworms had no hoarded supplies. My father's foresight had saved us from hunger and having to beg from others. But ours was a large family and the stockpile could not last for ever. Soon the flowers in our garden were replaced with tapioca, sweet potatoes and yams. The tapioca grew fast, and saved many from starvation.

As well as food, we had put away a hundred tins of Popo's favourite imported 555 cigarettes, but she was a heavy smoker and could get through a tin of fifty during a long session of *mah-jongg*. When she ran out, she had to turn to locally produced tobacco. It came in long fine dark-red strands, and its stench filled the house. She made do with it until early December when imported Japanese cigarettes became available. The kiosk near the police station opened for an hour on three mornings a week, and each customer was allowed ten cigarettes. On those days Popo would wake Miew-kin and me at six and send us in our pyjamas to join the queue. As soon as the kiosk's little window opened, the orderly line disintegrated. Everyone rushed forward and children were pushed to the back. Sometimes there were scuffles and unless we fought to stay at the front, we had little chance of buying even one cigarette.

Once the kiosk had sold out, touts hung around offering to sell the rations they had bought for much more than they had paid. But we didn't have enough money to buy on the black-market and often returned home empty-handed to face Popo's wrath. Some parents had complained to the man in the kiosk of the unfair advantage that adults had over children, but they were ignored. When my father heard what was going on, he told the police, and a uniformed officer was sent to tell the kiosk man to supervise the queue and make sure the cigarettes were fairly distributed.

Singapore had been occupied by the Japanese for several months when we began to prepare for the Chinese New Year and we were looking forward to the festival even more than usual: last year we had been living in fear of Japanese planes and there had been no celebration. It usually falls between 21 January and 19 February and goes on for a fortnight, with Chap Goh Meh, Fifteenth Night, marking the end. Before the war, the shops in Chinatown had overflowed with traditional delicacies imported from China, while Peranakan women had sold special cakes and other titbits. This year the shop-keepers could offer only what they had left from before the occupation, at steep prices, and Peranakans had no ingredients or fuel to bake their cakes.

Popo had started to prepare for New Year weeks in advance. 'We must celebrate as best we can,' she said to Mother. 'Who knows what things will be like next year?'

She set off for Chinatown, with Miew-kin and me to carry the shopping. First, she went to a narrow side-street where, on the pavement, men sat in chairs by their tables on which were laid portraits of gods, bright red paper, ink sticks and writing brushes. They set up stall only for New Year and wrote auspicious sayings and messages which, together with the gods' portraits, we bought each year and pasted up in our homes. Miew-kin and I waited patiently, without complaining, but after an hour we were relieved when Popo concluded her discussion with the calligrapher and he set to work with his ink and brushes.

Next on Popo's list was an item that every Chinese family had to have for the New Year prayers. Yearcakes were expensive because they had to be steamed for twelve hours, but we could not find any in the shops. Instead Popo bought candied winter melon, red and black pumpkin seeds and *bak-kwa* – pork that had been pounded until it was so thin it was almost transparent, then spread with honey and roasted.

When we got home and Mother saw that we had no yearcakes, disappointment was written on her face. She tasted the winter melon and pumpkin seeds, and said they were stale. 'Go back now and return them,' she told me, but Popo said the shopkeeper had warned her that he had had them for a year.

A week before New Year, Popo and Mother lit joss sticks and kowtowed to the gods, then took down the old portraits and sayings for burning. In Chinese mythology, this was the day on which the kitchen god, who lived in his portrait above the stove, would ascend to heaven to give an account of the family to the celestial emperor. A favourable one meant plenty to eat for the next year, and before she burnt the paper portrait Popo sprinkled sugar on the god's lips to sweeten his words. On the fourth day of the New Year, she would welcome him back when she pasted a new portrait of him above the stove.

The festival began on New Year's Eve with a family reunion dinner. For the next three days the Chinese shops would be closed while the workers spent their only paid holidays gambling and drinking, even those who normally did neither. The women would adorn themselves with all the gold, diamond and jade jewellery they had to command the respect and envy of others. Everyone would greet each other with the festive '*Kong hei fatt choy*,' good fortune and prosperity, while those who had fallen out during the year would take the opportunity to make up.

At dawn on New Year's Day, Popo and Mother left for the temple in a trishaw, the new bicycled carriage that was beginning to compete with the rickshaw. When they returned they were holding a lighted joss stick, 'bringing light to the household'. Red candles and more joss sticks burnt as we mumbled prayers to the gods, and the scent of sandalwood incense filled the house. When we had finished we went outside, where Father had lit a string of firecrackers that hung from a pole by the door and set off a series of bangs to ward off evil spirits.

After the last had exploded, Popo sat down in the sitting room and we children stood in line, each holding a cup of Chinese tea. One by one we knelt at her feet, wished her good fortune, gave her the tea and kowtowed. In return she gave us *hong pow*, a small red packet of money. I enjoyed the ceremony, but the best part was knowing that, for the next three days, we could play and eat without fear of beatings. The *muichai* were happier too because there could be no cleaning: if you used a broom at New Year you would sweep away good luck. My mother forbade crying or angry words because tears would bring sorrow in the New Year. A rare calm descended on our home.

During the festival we were allowed to eat the sweet rice from which Dai-chay had made the rice wine. Superstition governed the way in which the cooked glutinous rice, yeast and sugar were layered in the pot and menstruating women had to be kept away while it was prepared. Otherwise the wine would turn pink and sour. Popo was expert at making it and we liked to watch her pick up the cold cooked rice with her extra-long cooking chopsticks and sprinkle the yeast and sugar on top. One New Year Miew-kin went missing. As she never went out alone, we searched the house and eventually found her asleep in the servants' quarters. She was snoring and her breath smelt of liquor – she had eaten too much of the rice left over from the wine-making.

The first visitors to arrive on the second day of the festivities were Aunt Chiew-foong, Uncle Cong and their three children. Just a year ago they had refused us refuge from the bombs and I was surprised to see them because, in all that time, we had not been in touch. Children were taught not to take sides when adults quarrelled, so when I met Uncle Cong some months after he had turned us away I had greeted him politely. He had looked through me. Now he and his family looked tired and worn on our doorstep. We did not have to wait long to discover the reason for their visit.

Popo was overjoyed to see her younger daughter and grandchildren, and all was forgiven. My cousins sat quietly, eating whatever Popo put before them. Afterwards she encouraged them to rummage through our cupboards for clothes that would fit them.

Ten days later they came back. I answered a knock at the front door, expecting to see my parents' or Popo's friends, who appeared early in the morning at weekends to play *mah-jongg*, but Aunt Chiew-foong and Uncle Cong were on the doorstep. I was so surprised to see them again that I forgot to ask them in.

'Who's at the door?' Popo called, from the dining room where she was having breakfast.

Before I could reply, my uncle and aunt pushed past me and went into the dining room. Without waiting to be asked, they sat down and reached for some food. When they had finished eating, I saw Aunt Chiew-foong and Popo exchange a glance. Then they got up and went into the garden. I was curious and followed them, hanging back so they would not notice me. I sat down out of sight behind the henna tree.

'Why has your husband come with you to visit me?' Popo asked. 'It must be important for him to come again so soon.'

'We have no one else to turn to, Ma,' Aunt Chiew-foong blurted out. Then she lowered her voice, afraid that my mother would overhear: 'You are my last hope. The past months have been so hard – we don't get enough to eat.'

'Why didn't you come to me sooner?' Popo asked.

'Chiew-wah hasn't forgotten the bombing, when we wouldn't let you in. I had to wait for New Year to try to make up.'

'Didn't you buy food to store before the Japanese came?'

'Cong believes that buying food to store is a waste of money.'

'That husband of yours!' Popo shook her head. She had little respect for my father but she treated Uncle Cong with a degree of deference: he had earned her approval with his unyielding manner and refusal to help us.

'I've run out of money, buying on the black-market. What shall I do?' my aunt whined.

Popo had a soft spot for her younger daughter and now

she put an arm round her. 'I can't let you go hungry. I'll think of something, but Chiew-wah mustn't find out,' she said. 'Why aren't you wearing your jewellery for New Year?'

'The shops won't accept Straits Settlement dollars now, just Japanese money,' Aunt Chiew-foong said. 'They want jewellery. Everything you gave me is gone. I had to sell it or we would have starved.'

From then on, my aunt came to our house to eat three times a week at my father's expense. When she was expected, Dai-chay was told to cook extra. Often, when she had food in her mouth and her chopsticks were reaching for more, she would say that she didn't like what had been served. Afterwards she would leave without a word of thanks carrying a tiffin box of leftover food.

Soon after my aunt's visits began, Popo decided that the household expenses must be cut back. Dai-chay had always bought meat, fish and vegetables from the Orchard Road market, about half a mile away. It was the one that European women had preferred when they went shopping with their Chinese cook-boys and *amah*s. They had sat in comfortable chairs with their shopping lists while stall-holders brought them the freshest items to choose from. Then they had watched as the goods were packed into boxes and carried to the cars where the Malay drivers supervised the loading. Orchard Road was still the cleanest market with the best-quality food, but the prices were higher than at any other on the island. Another market at the top of Tanglin Road, near my school, catered mainly for local and *kampung* people; there the quality of the produce and the prices were lower.

'From now on, you will shop at the Tanglin Road market,' Popo said to Dai-chay.

'That market is an uphill walk,' Dai-chay argued. 'I'm so fat my legs won't carry me such a long way there and back with the shopping.'

In fact, the market was about the same distance as the one in Orchard Road, but when Popo insisted that she go there, Dai-chay threatened to leave: if she had to shop at the cheaper market, other professional cooks would laugh at her, she said. Dai-chay was too valuable to be allowed to leave, especially when so many were dropping in for free meals: she could devise ingenious ways of making food go further – she would add home-grown sweet potatoes to the rice, which was in short supply. Popo begged her to stay, and said that Sum-chay could shop at Tanglin market. But Sum-chay came from the same *coolie fong* as Dai-chay, and would not lower herself to go to the cheaper market. Popo was at her wit's end: she knew the *muichai* could not be trusted to do the shopping in case they ran away, and that Mother, with her long, painted fingernails, would not consider it. She asked her anyway but Mother was outraged. 'Let Miew-yong do it! She can ride the bicycle,' she snapped, pointing at me.

When my father came in from work and found out what was in store for me he was furious. 'Why do we need to cut back? I earn more than enough to keep us all,' he protested. 'Besides, Yong may be tall for her age but she is too young to carry heavy shopping. And if she has to leave school to do it, Beng must take her place there.' He hoped that his threat to send Beng to the Malay school would change her mind.

But Popo ignored the reference to Beng, and took offence. 'Are you saying I've been embezzling family funds? You think I'm a thief!'

Father backed down, muttered an apology and looked at me. I wanted to say that I knew why Popo had to reduce the shopping bill – I had seen her put money into Aunt Chiew-foong's pocket many times – but I didn't dare: Popo might burn my lips again with a lighted wick.

'Miew-yong can ride the bicycle with two baskets, one on each handlebar to balance the load,' Popo told Father. 'She can go to the market early in the morning, bring the food home, then go to school.'

I left early on the first day, at about six o'clock, in my school uniform and white canvas shoes. Yan-fok did the laces for me because they never stayed tied when I did them myself. School started at eight so, with a basket on each handlebar, I rode as fast as I could towards Tanglin Road and turned into the gravel path that led down to the market. It was not steep and my fingers were ready to grip the brakes. It wouldn't be easy pushing the bicycle back up with the shopping but I didn't want to think about that.

The smell of fish was in the air as I pushed the bicycle towards the fishmonger's stall. He stood behind stone tables piled with baby squid, live and wriggling; the fat prawns and small fish were covered with crushed ice to keep them fresh. Water from the stall trickled on to the floor and I realized my shoes would get wet and smelly – I would need to change them when I got home. Popo had told me to buy pork and chicken, whatever fresh fish was available, and eels, if there were any. I did not have a list but I wouldn't forget anything because that was what we ate every day. She told me the servants would deliver her *chap-ji-kee* stake to the grocer and buy the fruit and vegetables.

I couldn't see the better types of fish, like pomfret,

grouper and *ma-yau*, which was similar to the cod Dai-chay bought from the Orchard Road market and steamed with mushrooms and ginger. I watched a Malay woman select a dozen fish from a heap and hand them to the man. After she had paid I asked her what the fish were called and how to tell if they were fresh. She told me they were *ikan kuning* and that I should only buy them when their eyes were shiny. 'Deep-fry them and eat them with *sambal blachan*,' she said. I asked if she would help me choose the best, which she did. The fishmonger wrapped them, took my money and gave them to me to put in my basket.

I went on past the Indian mutton stall where I saw goats' heads, the eyes missing, on a table; the legs, shoulders and sides were hanging on hooks. I asked the stall-holder why the goats had no eyes, and he told me they were sold separately for hot pepper soup. The further inside I walked, the louder the noise of the market became and the more pungent the smell. Malay stall-keepers called, '*Beli dari sini! Sangat murah! Sangat murah!*' Buy from here! Very cheap! Very cheap! Bunches of dried fish and dried squid, slit and flattened with tentacles intact, and dried beans dangled from bars fixed across the front of the shops, and jute sacks of dried shrimps, dried anchovies, dried chillies, coriander, fennel, cumin and many other types of seed stood on the floor.

Next I went to the pork stall, bought what Popo wanted, then wheeled the bicycle on to the chicken stall. The birds were crammed into round rattan baskets on the floor and the air was acrid with the smell of droppings. There was a terracotta pot in the corner with a wooden cover, and next to it a stove with a pot of boiling water. Popo had told me to buy pullets that had laid no eggs and weighed up to a katty each. I asked for two and told the man, 'If you sell me the wrong sort my grandmother will return them.' I was afraid he would take advantage of me and that I would get into trouble for bringing back low-grade hens. He pulled a chicken out of a basket, caught both wings with one hand, held it upside down, blew the feathers to expose its bottom and put his finger inside. He shook his head, returned it to the basket, pulled out another and went through the same process. After two more attempts he had found the right one. He tied the hen's legs together, hooked it to a scale, weighed it and lifted it off. Then he folded the wings, pulled back the head, plucked some feathers from its throat and slit it with his knife. He threw the still-struggling chicken into the terracotta pot, then repeated the process with another. The chickens were scratching in the pot, and when the noise stopped he took them by their legs, dipped them in the boiling water, then held them under running water and plucked out their feathers.

I had no difficulty in pushing the bicycle up to the main road, but as soon as I got on, I fell off, then again, several times, until I had learnt to balance the baskets. When I got home, much later than I had planned, my knees were grazed and my white shoes dirty. I wondered how I would manage to do the shopping every day and still go to school, and remembered how my father had given in once again to Popo.

Seventeen

The Japanese worked Father hard as he was the only interpreter at the police station, and he often had to return in the evenings to finish his paperwork. My mother watched him leave with a jealous eye and became convinced he was up to something.

'If you must go back to the office every evening, you had better take Miew-kin or Miew-yong with you so that I can be sure you're not entertaining women,' she said.

She was suspicious, not because she loved Father but because she could not bear the idea of him being attracted to another woman. One evening, during a gathering at our house, a beautiful lady guest spent a lot of time talking to my father in various languages.

'Hmm! Look at your father and that woman,' Popo remarked to me, with a frown, 'laughing and talking in those devil languages. They're making your mother eat vinegar.'

I wanted to tell Popo that he was doing nothing wrong but I did not want to be slapped across the mouth in front of everyone. Popo never missed an opportunity to cause mischief. At the end of the party, when the guests had left, my mother, goaded by Popo, could no longer hold back her fury. She flew at my father, accusing him of flirting with the woman, and attacked him, ripping his shirt.

I became my father's chaperone when he went to his office in the evenings. I would make myself comfortable in a chair, reading my Malay schoolbooks, while he sat at his desk writing, muttering in different dialects, sometimes crumpling paper into balls and tossing them into the wastepaper basket. Soon he noticed that I was finding it hard to wake up in the morning so he decided to stop going into the office at night. He wanted to bring his work home but there was nowhere he could be out of earshot of Mother's outbursts and Popo's constant shouting at us girls. Instead, he went in at six in the morning.

By the middle of 1943, many were surviving on tapioca and sweet potatoes. Limbs swelled with beriberi, and Father showed us how to test for the disease by pressing a thigh or upper forearm with a finger, then quickly removing it. If the disease was present, the depression on the flesh would take longer than usual to flatten. He was worried that we might succumb to it and told Popo we must eat more fish so that we would get our vitamins.

Now that food was scarce and expensive, many people resorted to stealing vegetables and animals. The hundred or so chickens in our flock were let out of the coop in the morning and in the evening they would return to be fed. The old hens that had finished laying were slaughtered for the table, but the young ones supplied enough eggs each week for us and for Popo's *chimui* when they visited. As time went by, fewer and fewer hens emerged from the coop in the morning and we thought they must have strayed. Then, one day, we woke to find our vegetable garden trampled: torn leaves and children's footprints covered the ground and the yams, tapioca and sweet potatoes that had been ready to harvest had been stolen.

Also, the door to the chicken coop was open and the chickens were gone. My father refused to report the theft: 'It will only sour our friendly relationship with the *kampung* people,' he said. 'Besides, the people who stole our vegetables and chickens must be desperate, or they wouldn't have done it. We'll buy more hens and replant the vegetable patch.'

During the Japanese occupation those arrested for theft were beaten by Chinese, Malay and Indian detectives and locked up. The wives, mothers and sisters of men detained at the police station would mill about outside, pleading and wailing for their loved ones, only to be chased away by the officers. It was not in my father's nature to turn anyone away if they needed help and people knew this. Sometimes he would get home to find strangers outside the front door waiting for him.

Returning from school one day, I saw a woman and four children sitting on the kerb by the open drain at the entrance to our drive. The children were very thin and the woman's eyes were red and puffy. It was obvious that she had been crying. The children were sliding down the deep drain on their backsides and climbing up to do it again. It was constructed in a V shape and fun to play in – I liked to run up one side and down the other, or sit in the narrow bottom, hidden from view, when I wanted to escape Mother or Popo. It was safe on a fine dry day, but in a thunderstorm, it filled up in no time and animals or children who fell in couldn't climb out.

As soon as my father crossed the road from the police station, the woman called her children and together they knelt before him. 'Help us, I beg you,' she cried.

'Stand up,' Father said, taken aback. 'Up, up,' he said, waving his hand at the children. He disliked subservient

136

behaviour – I think it reminded him of Popo making Miew-kin and me kneel at her feet to be punished.

'My husband has been held at the police station for two days now. He stole a pig,' the woman told Father. 'I have already sold my furniture to feed my family,' she continued, blowing her nose. 'The last piece went several months ago and my husband still has no work. We don't eat every day and the children are always hungry.'

She told Father that they had to stand outside neighbours' houses at mealtimes and hope that someone would offer them a little leftover food but now their neighbours were nearly as poor as they were. Her husband had borrowed from a money-lender at high interest rates, knowing he had no means of repaying the debt without a job. Eventually he had resorted to stealing. 'He went to a nearby farm and stole a little pig, intending to sell it to pay the money-lender,' she said, covering her face with her hands.

He had tied the pig's legs, put it head first into a box and carried it away on the back of his bicycle. As he cycled along, the pig's squeals had aroused suspicion because live pigs were not often transported by bicycle. Usually they were crammed into rattan cages and stacked high on lorries. When a policeman had heard the squealing and stopped him, he could not explain how he had come by the pig.

'I have tried to see my husband to give him some food but they won't let me in and I fear that he has nothing to eat,' she said. She paused for a moment then added, 'I can hear the prisoners scream sometimes. I think the policemen beat him.' She showed Father a packet of cakes and begged him to give them to her husband. 'If I go to the station again, they will chase me away.'

I sat on the edge of the drain, trying to look as though

I wasn't listening – Popo punished eavesdropping – but my father knew I had heard every word. He looked at me and gestured to the woman. 'You know what to do,' he told me. Then, to her, he said, 'It is a small matter to take nourishment to your husband. What is his name?'

Father seldom refused to deliver food to prisoners but he never interfered when it came to the beatings. He could not risk being accused of subversion. When he was not at home and people arrived with food or begged help for their relatives, my mother would say to me, 'Don't bother with those people. We don't know them. They will forget that we have helped them when they are out of prison.' But I knew it would upset Father if I did nothing so I took the parcels to the prisoners without telling her. Now I set off with the cakes for the pig thief under my arm. As I crossed the road I wondered how it felt to have to steal to eat and whether, if my father lost his job, we would resort to theft and who we would turn to if Father was imprisoned.

No one objected to my presence at the police station because my father always made time for a word with the officers, gardeners and cleaners, and he was well liked. I had looked into the cells many times. Sometimes they were so full that there was hardly any room to move and then the prisoners could not sit down. Only a lucky few by the prison bars were able to get some fresh air. They all stripped to their underwear and dripped with perspiration. When I reached the police station I gave the pig thief's name to an officer and he called it out. A thin prisoner pushed his way towards the bars. 'Here,' I said, handing him the food. 'Your wife and children are at my house.' He gave a big smile and thanked me profusely, but I told him to thank my father, not me.

On my way back through the compound a shrill cry startled me. I was curious to know where it had come from and what kind of animal had made the noise so I looked under the cars and lorries. I heard another squeal. It came from a box lying on the Tarmac in the full heat of the sun. When the box squealed again I forced the lid up, peeped inside and saw a piglet, its legs bound and bleeding because it was struggling to free itself. I decided to pull the box to the shade of the hibiscus hedge a few feet away but it was too heavy for me to move it far. The frightened animal squealed again. I needed help, but I could not ask the Malay policemen's children to help me because they would not touch a pig. Their religion forbade it. At last I remembered Tamby, our Indian gardener. I found some water, poured it over the box and ran home to look for him.

Tamby, a native of Calcutta, was tall and muscular – he liked to show off his big biceps – and his skin was the colour of charcoal. Instead of using a toothbrush he chewed a stick and his teeth gleamed white. He always wore a vest and shorts, his feet bare, and sometimes arrived for work with a red spot painted on his forehead. My father allowed him to pick fruit from the garden for his family, but he only ever took the tip of the large flower spike on the banana tree. His wife made curry with it and he always returned with a large dish for us, which Popo accepted but threw away later. That day I found Tamby spreading animal dung round the gladioli and spider orchids and begged him to help the hot, frightened piglet. Eventually he followed me across the road. He carried the box to the foot of the hedge where he opened it, cut the string that bound the piglet's legs, then he waited while I poured more water over the box. I replaced the lid and covered it with banana leaves I had brought from the garden.

I told Father about the piglet, and the next day when he came home for lunch he told me that an angry, thickset man called Ong had turned up at the police station claiming to own it. He had been swearing and shaking his finger at the officers for not patrolling his area so that a thief had been able to steal his piglet. One of the officers had cautioned him, but Ong had continued his tirade. Then a policeman holding a pair of handcuffs had placed a hand on his shoulder. 'We always carry out our patrols so you are making false accusations. We're going to arrest you.' Once Ong was handcuffed, he apologized repeatedly. He hadn't meant to insult anyone, he said, and begged the policemen to let him go. It was then that Father saw an opportunity to help the pig thief and decided, for once, to interfere.

He asked the policeman to remove the handcuffs, then led Ong into his office. 'The man who stole from you had no choice but to do so because his children are starving and he can't find work. You may have your pig back, but you will still face a charge of slandering the police.'

Ong looked terrified. 'I want to drop my complaint and forget about the whole thing,' he said.

'It's not as simple as that,' Father said. 'You came into the station and made an accusation against the police and now you want them to forget it? It's a very serious matter.'

Ong took some money from his pocket and laid it on the table. 'This is for you.'

'Put it away. You'll get into even more trouble if you try to bribe me.'

Worry lines creased Ong's forehead. 'I'm a sick man,' he said. 'Who will look after my animals if I go to jail?'

'I can try to talk to the policemen you insulted and ask them to drop the charges – on one condition.'

'I will agree to anything – anything at all,' said Ong.

A few weeks later the pig thief's wife and four children came to thank my father. The woman was all smiles as she told Father that her husband was now working for the pig owner and her children had enough to eat.

Eighteen

When Father arrived at his office one morning two new faces greeted him. They belonged to Lye, his new assistant, and Andrew, a clerk. Father was always friendly and trusting but, as he later admitted, he was not a good judge of character. He welcomed them both without suspecting that, before long, they would repay his kindness with treachery.

On one of our Sunday visits to the Chinese restaurant I asked Father how his new assistant was getting on. He told me that Lye had not settled in very well. The day before he had arrived late but had not apologized. Instead he had complained that the police station was a long way to cycle from his home. As the day had worn on, he had muttered and moaned so much that Father had sat him down and asked him what was really troubling him.

'I am over forty, older than you and as qualified as you are, so I am losing face by taking orders from you,' Lye said. 'Perhaps my family and I can move in with you until I can find a place nearby. It will save me a lot of time every day.'

'Impossible,' replied my father. 'I have five children and you have four teenagers. My house isn't big enough for two families. Ask the Japanese officer if you can transfer back to the district you came from.'

But Lye did not have the nerve to approach the Japanese officers and, as the weeks passed, he became increasingly difficult and resentful.

Andrew, the junior clerk, was in his early twenties, a cheerful young man who always grinned before he spoke. Taller than my father, he liked to wear loose white shirts and baggy white trousers two sizes too big. He had lost both parents very young and my father, who felt sorry for him, often put in a good word for him with the senior officers. Soon, Father was treating him like a member of our family, introducing him to his friends and often bringing him home for lunch. 'A nice young man, bright and intelligent,' was how he described him. Andrew spent a lot of time at our house and I became a little jealous, although I was glad to see Father happy. Popo had come between him and his own sons so he rarely spent time with them. Now a stranger had filled the gap in his heart.

Our entire household, including the servants, were fond of Andrew. We children were told to call him Brother, and after he had played several card games with Mother, Popo and Dai-chay, he would sometimes stay the night. He seldom spoke of his family, and it was as if his parents had never existed. His grandfather was mother and father to him and they lived above their liquor shop selling *samsu*, the only drink available during the occupation. Popo told him that she much preferred the light-brown *samsu* to her home-made rice wine. 'It has a stronger kick,' she said. 'It is just like the *samshui* we used to make in China from millet and molasses.'

Even though he now had an assistant, Father continued to work long hours at the police station. I liked to have him to myself, away from my mother and Popo, so I would go to meet him at the police station in the evenings and walk home with him. As I waited in the shade of the trees outside I had a clear view of the entrance to the detectives' offices, and often saw handcuffed prisoners being brought in, then going out with bruises.

One evening when Father had not appeared after I had been there for nearly an hour, I worried that I would be told to go away and I crawled into a bush where I could wait for him unseen. It was hot, and I fell asleep. Suddenly a shout woke me. When I opened my eyes I saw, through the bush, a middle-aged Chinese man in his underpants with his hands cuffed behind his back, kneeling by the swing door a few yards from my hiding-place. Two detectives were kicking him while a *kempetai*, a Japanese military policeman, in civilian clothes with badges pinned to his jacket, stood watching with a truncheon in his hand.

'Who has a wireless? Tell us and we'll stop hitting you,' said the *kempetai*.

The man bowed his head to the floor. 'I swear I do not know who has a wireless!'

The truncheon went down on his head, followed by more kicking. The smell of urine and excrement filled the air but the policemen continued to beat the man. When they stopped one of the detectives went to a hosepipe and turned it on to wash the ground. I could hardly breathe – but worse was to come. One detective held the Chinese man down while the other forced the hose into his mouth. He squirmed and struggled but gradually his stomach swelled. Then the first detective picked up a board that was propped against the wall, placed it over the man's stomach and jumped on it, hard. The man stopped struggling and lay still. He didn't move again. The *kempetai* turned and walked away, leaving the two detectives standing by the man's body.

I was too frightened to move so I stayed hidden in the bush until it was dark. As I watched the policemen come and go through the swing door I kept thinking of Father's wireless in its secret compartment and what would happen if the Japanese discovered it.

The next day I told Father what I had seen and heard. 'The wireless is the only way to know what is happening in the war, but you're right. The family cannot be put at risk,' he said.

I was drawn to the same hiding-place again and again as I waited for my father to finish work and watched prisoners being beaten, subjected to water torture and having wires inserted under their fingers and toenails. Some endured the pain with dignity, protesting that they had been falsely accused by their enemies, while others begged, but their denials and pleadings made no difference. I wondered how such a thin piece of wire could make a grown man scream in such agony.

I had grown used to the sight of dead or injured people and the hordes of starving refugees on the pavements. On my way to school in the morning I passed beggars sleeping by the roadside, their legs covered with sores and flies, and every week Japanese soldiers with bayonets fixed to their rifles would march European prisoners, in khaki shorts and muddy shoes, along our road. Each man carried a hoe over his shoulder and looked emaciated, cheeks sunken, eyes staring blankly, sunburnt red skin draped over protruding ribs. Popo called them the 'walking skeletons'. The atrocities I witnessed outside the police station no longer shocked me.

At home, I hid my feelings as I endured Mother and Popo's punishments. Often Miew-kin and I were beaten in front of visitors, who turned a blind eye: they didn't want to jeopardize the hospitality they enjoyed. Many even agreed that it was the correct Oriental way to discipline children. 'They must be beaten into obedience,' one woman said, between mouthfuls of the *char sui* she had not tasted since the Japanese had arrived.

I looked forward to festival days because my mother and grandmother were less likely to hit me. The mid-autumn festival, honouring the moon goddess, Ch'ang O, falls on the fifteenth day of the eighth lunar month in the Chinese calendar and is observed by the giving and receiving of moon cakes and, for children, paper lanterns in the shape of fruit, animals, aeroplanes and ships. In September 1944, on the night of the full moon, Popo held a moon-watching party in the garden with moon cakes, buns and candle-lit lanterns. That night we stayed up late, playing in the garden, and eating the cakes in the light of the moon, and went to bed happy and content.

The next morning, Dai-chay did not appear at the usual time for breakfast. Sum-chay thought she must be tired after all the hard work she had put into preparing the festival food, so she left her to sleep. After lunch when she had still not emerged from her room Sum-chay, ironing a pair of trousers, looked at the clock. 'Time she was up to make dinner.' She went to the servants' quarters and shook Dai-chay. She could not wake her. Then she felt her forehead. It was cold. Dai-chay was lying on her side so Sum-chay turned her over. Then she screamed and ran out of the room.

Sum-chay related her story to us as we sat glumly in the kitchen after Father had told us that Dai-chay had died from a heart-attack. I would never hear her voice again or run from her flapping arms as she chased us out of the kitchen, I thought. After her body had been taken away, Sum-chay and the two *muichai* were afraid to sleep in her room, which they had shared, and persuaded Popo to let them sleep in the spare room, next to mine. Sum-chay had done little cooking before now, but she began to prepare simple meals that were far from the sumptuous dishes Dai-chay had made. Miew-kin and I took turns to help in the kitchen, while the *muichai* cleaned the house and did the laundry.

Sum-chay's cooking was limited to stewed pork, stewed chicken with ginger and dark soy, steamed fish with ginger and crushed yellow beans, and meat with stir-fried vegetables, which were either overcooked and mushy or almost raw. Sometimes Popo would roll up her sleeves to prepare her favourite beef and broccoli leaves. She would cross-cut a piece of steak into thin slices, season it with grated ginger, light soy, sugar, cornflower, sesame oil and a drop of brandy, then leave it to stand. Later she heated oil and garlic in the wok until it was smoking, then put in the meat. As it touched the sides, flames would shoot out of the wok. At the last minute she would throw in the finely-cut vegetables and it was ready. 'This is the way I like it – the beef soft and tender, the vegetables green and crisp,' she would say proudly.

One evening Sum-chay made stewed pork and steamed mullet. The best of the fish was given to Beng, Sai-ngau and Wang-lai, of course, and I was not keen on stewed pork. However, I had to eat something, so I spooned some bony fish and bean sauce over my bowl of rice, careful not to spill any on the table – if I did I was hit over the head with Popo's chopsticks. I removed the bones, placed them on my saucer and remembered to eat with my mouth closed. Across the table my mother was sucking the bones and spitting them on to her saucer. From the corner of my eye I saw her raise her chopsticks and hit Wang-lai. 'Stop playing with your rice. It's all over the table,' she ordered. Tears ran down my little sister's face and dripped into her bowl.

I knew that Mother would pick on me next and I gobbled the rest of my food so that I could leave the table. Suddenly I was choking. I dropped my bowl and chopsticks on the table and gasped, 'A bone in my throat!'

Popo got up calmly, went to the rice pot, scooped out a tablespoon of hot rice, put it into the palm of her hand and squeezed it into a ball. 'Open wide and swallow,' she said, and pushed it into my mouth. 'Don't chew,' she ordered. The hot riceball dislodged the bone and I could breathe again.

By November, the monsoon had begun. Since we had been at war, the drains and canals that carried rainwater to the sea had been half filled with rubbish, and low-lying streets were often several feet deep in water. After it had rained for two days and nights the drains that ran along both sides of Orchard Road could take no more and neighbouring streets were flooded. Our garden disappeared under a lake. That evening my father carried his shoes and rolled up his trousers to wade knee deep through the flood to our house. Two beggars were taking shelter by the steps to the front door and he greeted them with a nod.

I had been watching him cross the road and when he came in I took my place at the table. Usually he asked for food to be taken outside if beggars were waiting and they sat on the steps to eat it. But the water had crept up the steps and was almost seeping into the house, so he called them in to eat with us. They walked in uncertainly, but Father made them welcome and positioned two chairs at the opposite end of the table from which my mother was sitting.

'What are they doing at the table? Why can't they eat outside?' she asked, annoyed.

He ignored her and summoned Sum-chay, whom he asked to bring in two large bowls of rice. There was silence. The smell of sweat and unwashed bodies was overpowering. I put down my chopsticks and covered my nose with both hands. My brothers and sisters did the same.

Father frowned. 'Where are your manners?' he asked.

Reluctantly we put down our hands and sat silently while he talked to the beggars and piled food into their bowls. My mother did not touch hers. Instead she lit a cigarette, took several puffs in quick succession and sat stonily, trying to control herself. Then, slowly, she began to spoon soup into her rice. When the bowl was full she stood up and glared at Father, who was sitting next to her. Suddenly she picked it up and emptied it over his head. With the other hand, she swept the dishes nearest her on to the floor. 'Don't invite beggars to sit at my dinner table again. Next time it will be worse,' she said, through clenched teeth.

Rice and soup ran down Father's face. I wasn't surprised by my mother's outburst: they were a regular mealtime occurrence. A wrong word from Father, Miew-kin or me would spark off a tantrum. This time my father did not move. A moment later, she flew at him. Broken crockery and food littered the floor as she screamed at him and beat him with both fists. When she paused for breath, Father got up, went into the bathroom and shut the door.

The beggars were dumbfounded and gaped at Mother, open mouths filled with half-chewed food, as if they had never before seen a woman behave like that. In spite of the pandemonium, though, they didn't want to leave the table and carried on eating until Mother picked up another bowl and threatened to throw it at them if they did not leave. They leapt out of their chairs and ran for the front door.

With the beggars gone Mother went on throwing bowls and dishes at the door, the walls and through the windows. Eventually she stormed out of the room.

I could hear Father having a bath. Some time later he emerged, dressed, went to the front door, rolled up his trousers and picked up his shoes. He went out and, from the house, I watched him plough through the water towards the police station. He had lost face in front of strangers and must be hurt and humiliated by what had happened, I thought. I was worried about him, but I was scared to follow him through the flood. Anyway, it was dark outside and it had begun to rain again, big drops splashing into the black lake.

I went to find Miew-kin who had fled the dining room during the fracas, and begged her to go with me after Father.

'There will be more trouble if Mother finds us missing,' she said.

'But we must find him!'

'I'm not going,' she said. 'It's so dark – what if we fall into the drain and drown? Mother would blame him.'

I was tempted to call Beng to walk with me, but I couldn't trust him to keep a secret. Hoping Miew-kin would change her mind, I whispered, 'I'll wait for you outside the front door.'

After I had stood there for nearly half an hour, watching the storm, I went inside and found Miew-kin in her pyjamas giving Popo a massage. My heart sank. I went back to the steps and wondered what to do. I could see the light from Father's office cutting a faint path across the water and worry overcame my fear of walking across a flooded road in the dark. I found a broom, took off my slippers, opened the door and stepped into the water. It came up to my knees. The wind and rain pounded on the fan palm trees in our neighbours' front garden and the huge leaves fluttered. It was so dark that I couldn't see the house next door clearly, just a faint glimmer through the cracks in the shutters.

Splash! A tree fell into the water – banana or papaya, because they were not strong.

As I inched my way forward, leaves hit my face and rain soaked my hair, but I was not cold. I waded down the drive to the road, my eyes fixed on the faint streaks of light coming through the shutters of the policemen's living quarters opposite.

I reached the hibiscus hedge that edged our garden where the drive went over the storm drain. The narrow crossing was under water and there were no handrails to steady me. I could hear the water gushing down the drain and I hesitated, afraid I would fall in. A lightning bolt lit up the sky and I moved to the centre of the crossing. I used the broom to feel the ground beneath me, then I waited for the next bolt to show me the rest of the way. It took me a long time to travel four feet across the drain, but once I was over, I felt safer, and waded on through the flood.

Without a sound, I went into Father's office. I stood by the door and watched him for several minutes before he saw me. He was sitting with his head resting in his hands. I had never seen him cry before and thought how old and tired he looked, although he was only thirty-one. A number of empty bottles stood on the table. He lifted his head, got to his feet and staggered to the cupboard for another. On his way back to the table he stumbled and caught my eye. I wanted to rush to him and hug him, but fathers did not show affection for their daughters like that, so I could tell him I loved him only with my eyes.

He refilled his glass with a shaking hand. I could see several more bottles in the cupboard and realized, with alarm, that he had been drinking secretly in his office. At home, except on special days, he hardly touched liquor. Popo and her friends chatted while they played *mah-jongg* and from their conversations I knew people died from drinking too much of the locally-made *samsu*. Some made it using dirty tins and bottles. I hoped Father was drinking the clean sort and wondered how long he had been drinking, but it would have been disrespectful to ask.

I did not speak to him until after he had ordered coffee from the canteen, which stayed open until midnight. I waited for him to drink it, then asked softly, 'Father, why do you allow Popo and Mother to treat you so badly? Why must Popo stay with us all the time and not with Aunt Chiew-foong and Uncle Cong?'

For a while, he did not reply and I wasn't sure if he had heard me. At last he said, 'Popo came to my rescue when your mother, Beng and I were driven from our home after my mother died. I had no one to turn to, except Popo.'

I thought of Fat Lum and his treachery towards the boy he had pretended to love, about Popo and her demand that Father should never visit his mother Kum Tai's grave, and about Mother who did not love him.

Father sat up, filled his glass, then broke down and cried again. 'I don't know how much more I can take.'

I wanted to cry with him, but I was too angry: angry with Popo and my mother for humiliating him, and angry with my father for drinking. He went on until the bottle was empty, then dozed in his chair. As the storm raged outside, I kept a silent vigil.

When Father woke, the rain had ceased and the wind had dropped. Outside the flood had subsided a little. He smiled and beckoned to me and together we went out into the moonless night and a landscape swept clean by lashing rain. I slipped my hand into his as we walked home.

Nineteen

Andrew knew how to charm Popo: he had seen that she enjoyed a drink with dinner and brought her *samsu* from his grandfather's shop. Almost every day, at lunchtime and after work, he made himself at home with us, even taking naps on our beds. Sometimes he went to the back garden to tease the *muichai* as they did their chores.

Ah-pin had been a plain, skinny twelve-year-old when Popo bought her from Gasbag Wong. Nearly four years on, she had grown into a beautiful shapely girl, with large almond eyes shaded by long black lashes. She was not allowed to use makeup, or even talcum powder when she suffered from prickly heat, yet her dark skin was rich and smooth. Popo often remarked that Ah-pin must be only half Chinese because her skin was so dark and her lashes so long. Sitting by the window, I watched Ah-pin take the washing off the clothes line, fold each piece carefully and put it into the wicker basket. As she reached up for the handkerchiefs, Andrew ran up behind her and put his hands on her breasts. She shouted and struggled, but he continued to fondle her until I climbed out of the window and ran towards them. He turned to look at me, red-faced and abashed. 'Mind your own business,' he said, then laughed. He tightened his arms round Ah-pin, then let go with such a sharp push that she fell over.

I bent down to help her up. She was crying quietly as she told me that this was not the first time Andrew had touched her and that she had never dared to complain because everyone liked him and she was sure she would be accused of lying. I suggested we tell Popo straight away. 'She'll believe you if we tell her together,' I said, glaring at Andrew.

Andrew grinned. 'Go on then. Tell Popo. Do you really think she'll take your word against mine?'

He was right. Popo didn't believe us. Andrew had told her that his grandfather was a wealthy man: 'I wouldn't stoop so low as to molest a *muichai*. Some day I will inherit everything, including the liquor shop. I can't understand why she lied,' he said.

Popo was impressed by his wealth and as he was acting as if he had been wronged, she reached for her rattan cane, took hold of Ah-Pin and gave her ten strokes. Then she turned to me. I always crouched when Popo or Mother beat me so that the stick landed on my back and didn't mark my arms and legs, but I wasn't going to bend my knees with Andrew looking on. All I could think of as Popo hit me was that she had done a great injustice: she was punishing me for trying to protect Ah-pin. It was worse than anything she had done before, worse even than when she had bound me to the teak table and pressed a lighted wick to my mouth. With each slash of her cane, my respect for her died a little until it was gone. Neither Ah-pin nor I shed a tear.

In the morning, my arms and legs were covered with red stripes. I didn't want to be teased at school, so I put a warm compress on my skin, hoping to reduce the redness, but the marks became even redder and I was too embarrassed to go to school – yet I had to leave the house or I would be in even more trouble. I liked school and had never been absent before, but I felt I had no alternative. I stayed away for two days, passing the time near the mango trees. In the thicket that surrounded them I found wild sugar cane to quench my thirst and watched the chameleons crawling on the branches, changing colour in the sunlight and darting out their long tongues to catch insects. We were not allowed to keep pets, or I would have brought a few home.

Popo had told us stories about her village in Canton, where most animals were considered edible, so if I had taken them home, they would have been killed. It seemed normal for her to kill monkeys, dogs, cats, lizards and snakes so that she could cook them with herbs. Among Popo and Mother's friends, I had never come across any who kept pets, except Mrs Low, one of Popo's closest *chimui*.

Mrs Low lived with her daughter Li-lan, her son-in-law Boon and her two grandchildren in Keppel Road, near the city's deep-water harbour. Whenever I knew that Popo planned to visit her, I would beg to go too because the family had a puppy. Popo would spend hours gossiping with Mrs Low and her daughter, so I played with the puppy.

One day, after Popo had recovered from a cough and aching bones, she was keen to catch up with Mrs Low and said I could go with her. When we arrived at the house the puppy seemed smaller than it had on my last visit, and thereafter it grew no bigger and was just as playful. One day, in the rickshaw on our way home, I could no longer contain my curiosity. 'Is there something wrong with Mrs Low's puppy?' I asked. 'Why doesn't it grow?'

Popo looked at me sideways. 'The meat is sweet and

tender when they are young. They ate the last one. The puppy you saw today will be killed when it's a little heavier. Mrs Low wouldn't waste money on keeping a pet.'

We had had lunch at Mrs Low's house and there had been several meat dishes. As Popo's words sank in, I felt sick and threw up on the floor of the rickshaw. Then I asked, 'Did we eat dog meat?'

'You stupid girl, of course we didn't.'

'Are you sure? We had stir-fried meat with spring onions.'

Popo knew I would persist in questioning her, so she decided to tell me the whole story. But first she issued a warning.

'Even Mrs Low's grandchildren don't know that their mother feeds dog to their father.'

'I won't say anything,' I promised.

'It's hard to find a black dog like that – and very expensive,' said Popo, and proceeded to tell me why Mrs Low and Li-lan had gone to all the trouble of finding one identical black puppy after another. It concerned Li-lan's husband, Boon. As a detective, he dealt with gangsters, pimps and prostitutes. He was always honest and fair-minded, and he could never be persuaded to turn a blind eye. He had met a woman at a friend's birthday party and become friendly with her. A few weeks later, she invited him to dinner at her home. He drank so much that he couldn't ride his motorbike home and stayed the night with her. The next morning he told Li-lan he had been working all night, and she believed him because he had always been faithful. Then he began to stay away for two, sometimes three nights in a week, claiming he had been at work. Li-lan believed him and was concerned that he had to put in such long hours.

One evening, Li-lan had been at the amusement park with a few friends. When she left, she spotted her husband in the crowd ahead of her, holding a middle-aged woman's hand. She followed them to the car park and confronted them. Boon brushed her off, got on to his motorbike with the other woman and rode away. He did not come home for several days, and when he returned, he accused Li-lan of spying on him and threatened to move out to live with his concubine. She pleaded with him not to leave her and promised that she would never again challenge him in public. He told her that from now on he would spend three nights a week away and four at home.

Li-lan had to agree or lose him, but she was furious. Then she decided that the woman had cast a spell on him – she was older than Li-lan and unattractive.

The use of magic to ensnare a member of the opposite sex, and to reverse the effects, was the province of the *bomoh*, and many sought their services as a matter of course. They did not advertise so their customers came across them by word of mouth. Popo told me that Mrs Low and Li-lan had decided against using one to reverse the effects of the spell on Boon as they were Taoists, with a deep belief in ancestor worship, and thought that magic meant asking help from demons. Instead Li-lan confided in her best friend, who told her that the meat of an all-black male dog could protect one against a spell. Li-lan ordered a black puppy, took it home and killed it. Then she made it into a hot curry, which she served to her husband. She passed off the meat as beef.

After that, whenever I heard Popo gossiping to her *chimui* about Mrs Low my ears pricked up. That was how I found out what had happened to Li-lan and Boon. Almost a year after Li-lan had bought the first black puppy, there was no sign that the dog meat had had any effect on her husband – by then he'd found a second woman, younger than the first, and was seeing his family only at weekends. She continued to feed him the meat, hoping that it would eventually cure him. Her plan backfired when Boon began to pass blood. Somehow his parents discovered that their son had been fed dog meat, and accused Li-lan of trying to poison him. In the end she lost both him and her children.

The marks from Popo's cane faded, but Andrew did not stop pestering Ah-pin. Whenever he thought no one was looking, he would rub himself against her and pinch her behind. She dared not utter a word but sometimes I would hear a muffled cry and know what he had done. I dared not speak against him now, though, for fear of another beating from Popo. Whenever he looked my way I showed him with my eyes what I thought of him. Soon he began to molest our other *muichai*, Yan-fok. She was small with beautiful white teeth and looked fragile. She did not try to stop him – she remembered the ten strokes Ah-pin and I had received for complaining about him – but she kept out of his way as far as she could. Andrew was incapable of keeping his hands to himself. He even persuaded my mother to teach him ballroom dancing – when my father was out – and held her so tightly that even the servants tutted under their breath.

I knew that Andrew was attracted to the *muichai* but I was entirely ignorant of the 'facts of life': the mere mention of such matters was viewed as 'dirty talk'. Once when I asked Popo how my mother had given birth to me, she said, 'One afternoon when she was walking on a country lane, a boulder exploded and she found you inside.' I didn't believe her – my father had taken me to the hospital to visit Mother when Kwai-chan was born. When I reminded Popo of this, she said, 'Kwai-chan was found inside a boulder, too, but your mother took her to the hospital. Stop asking questions.'

Late one evening, after dinner, Andrew complained of a headache and said he felt too ill to go home. 'I'll sleep on the veranda sofa,' he said. Popo made him some herbal tea and fussed over him, then left him to sleep. In spite of the heat, our house had no ceiling fans – Popo didn't want to waste electricity – so some windows were left open at night. The room where the servants slept led off the veranda. Just after midnight I was woken by an ear-splitting scream. Miew-kin and I jumped out of bed, hearts beating wildly, and ran to the servants' quarters, closely followed by Popo.

Popo rushed into the room, followed by Father. Sum-chay was sitting up in bed, pointing at Andrew, who was struggling to get dressed next to the mattress where Ah-pin lay. Breathlessly, she told Father that she had heard noises and had turned on the light to find Andrew, naked, lying on top of Ah-pin. Father ushered Miew-kin and me out of the room and closed the door behind us.

Then we heard Father's voice. It was clear that he was angry. He told Andrew that he had considered him part of the family and couldn't believe how he had misjudged him. 'Such a dishonourable act,' he said.

Then we heard Sum-chay accuse Andrew of planning to rape Ah-pin – I wondered what she meant. 'He knew that the windows of the house were left open on hot, humid nights,' she said, 'and he found out which Ah-pin's mattress was. He asked me how far apart we slept. I'd no idea why he was so interested.'

'You have abused our hospitality, Andrew. Get dressed

and leave immediately,' Father barked. 'I will deal with you in the morning.'

'Popo,' we heard Andrew say, 'if you tell people I raped a *muichai*, my reputation will be gone.'

'Your reputation! After what you've done?' Father said.

'My chances of marrying into a decent family will be ruined,' Andrew continued, as if he hadn't heard what my father had said. 'And if Grandfather comes to know about it, the shock may kill him.'

Then he tried to pin the blame on Ah-pin. 'She enticed me into the room,' he said. 'She wanted me to marry her so she can be free of your family.'

Inside the room everyone began to talk at once and Ah-pin was crying. Andrew kept repeating his story and blaming Ah-pin until my father did not know who to believe, but Popo had already concluded that Ah-pin was the guilty party. 'She has tried to use Andrew to gain her freedom,' she declared, and told Andrew she would decide on Ah-pin's punishment in the morning.

As Popo opened the door we saw Ah-pin huddled on her mattress, shivering. Then Popo led Andrew back to the veranda, saying, 'It is too late for you to go home now.'

But Father put his foot down. 'No! You must leave and stay away from my house,' he said.

The days that followed brought more wretchedness to Ah-pin as my grandmother made her pay for what Andrew had done. The following morning she was beaten and made to kneel in a tray of sand until her knees bled. Popo would not believe that a wealthy, educated, good-looking young man like Andrew could have any-thing to do with a *muichai* unless he had been seduced. 'Do you think he wants you, a *muichai*, to carry his child?'

she asked. And no matter how much Ah-pin protested her innocence, begged for mercy and pleaded not to be sent away, Popo took no notice. Mother joined in with the punishment, kicking Ah-pin as she knelt in the sand.

That night Popo did not go straight to bed. She went to the altar, took her beads from the altar drawer and sat down to meditate. When she had finished she called Ah-pin to her and said, 'You should pray that you are not with child. If you are, no one will want you.'

Lying on my mattress next to Miew-kin, I thought about what Popo had said to Ah-pin and wondered what happened when a girl was raped. I decided to ask Ah-pin what Andrew had done to her. The next day when she went to hang out the washing I followed her. I watched as she pegged the wet clothes to the line and saw the livid streaks on her arms. When she had finished, I glanced about to make sure that no one was within ear-shot, and asked her to tell me what had happened that night. She told me she had tried to push Andrew off but he was too strong for her. Then she described what he had done to her, and started to cry. 'I have done nothing wrong but your mother and grandmother beat me so much and they haven't finished with me yet,' she said. I saw on her face the terror of the child whom Gasbag Wong had brought to our house and who had knelt in rags before Popo.

From then on, Ah-pin cleaned the house, washed the pots and folded our clothes as if she was in a trance, while she waited for her mistress to decide her fate.

Twenty

Popo and my mother deliberated for a long time about what to do with Ah-pin, but they could not reach a decision. One morning, after Father had left for work, Mother suggested that Ah-pin should go to Aunt Chiew-foong. 'That will be punishment enough,' she said, with an unkind smile.

'No, Chiew-wah. They will talk about me behind my back,' Popo replied. She was referring to her *chimui* and I knew she was thinking about Ah-pin's cousin, Ah-yuen, whom she had sent to my aunt to help her with her baby. As Aunt Chiew-foong's family had grown, Ah-yuen was made to help in the kitchen, clean the house and do all the laundry, as well as caring for the children. She was never allowed out of the house and when she was slow with her chores or did not come quickly enough when she was called, my aunt would twist her ear, pinch the underside of her arm or slap her face.

When Popo took me with her to visit my aunt in Rangoon Road, Ah-yuen was always pleased to see me. She would ask about her cousin: 'Is Ah-pin beaten often by your mother and grandmother? Does she have enough to eat?' She asked the same questions each time, then told me how much she wanted to come to our house to see her cousin, but my aunt would not let her go. The two girls had not seen or spoken to each other since they were parted. When I got home, Ah-pin would be waiting for news of her cousin.

Ah-yuen always wore a tattered, ill-fitting *samfoo*, her blouse in one print and the trousers in another. Thin, with sunken cheeks, she looked starved but she bore her lot as best she could. She knew that as her parents had sold her into slavery she had no choice but to accept whatever was handed out to her, but she hoped that, one day, she would be free to marry, have her own family and find her parents. Even Popo, hard-hearted as she was, commented on Ah-yuen's poor condition and torn clothes. But my aunt said, 'Ma, she is only a *muichai*. How do you expect me to dress her?' Popo smiled patiently and let the matter drop, but she could not forget about it. She was sure people were talking about the skinny *muichai* whom my aunt dressed in rags.

Occasionally Popo brought some of my mother's old clothes for Ah-yuen – 'It is indecent for a young girl's flesh to be seen' – and although she had no reservations about the beatings – she probably beat me a lot more often and harder – she felt strongly that the overworked *muichai* should have enough to eat. Popo was superstitious, and disturbed by the idea that Ah-yuen might die of starvation to come back as a ghost and haunt her. However, she didn't want to deprive my aunt of a servant by taking her back to our house.

I found out how little Ah-yuen was given to eat on one of our visits. My aunt had a guava tree in her garden and the fruit was ripe and yellow. I was sure she wouldn't mind if I picked a few – she was quick to help herself to anything she wanted at our house. I was circling the tree with a bamboo pole, ready to hit a laden branch, when

Ah-yuen ran out of the kitchen, waving frantically. 'Don't pick the guavas,' she called.

'Why not?' I said.

'I'll get the blame if any are missing.' She put a hand on my arm and whispered, 'I have something to tell you,' then led me to the far end of the garden. She rolled up her sleeves to reveal black-and-blue bruises on both arms. 'My whole body is like this,' she said, plainly fighting back tears.

She told me that she was always hungry because she was only given what was left after Aunt Chiew-foong and her family had finished a meal. On a good day, there might be a chicken wing or a fish head with some sauce, but on other days, when they had bought roast duck or pork, there would be nothing, not even sauce. One evening she had gone to bed on an empty stomach. When she woke, early the next morning, she had been so hungry that she had picked two guavas and eaten them. She hadn't known that my aunt kept count of the fruit on the tree. Later, Aunt Chiew-foong had checked the tree and found two guavas missing. At first she thought that they had been blown down by the wind and searched the garden. When she didn't find them she had pointed the finger at Ah-yuen, who, fearing the worst, denied having eaten them. But Aunt Chiew-foong had suspected she was lying. She had brought a basin and made Ah-yuen tickle her throat with her finger until she vomited. There were pieces of half-digested guava in the basin and Ah-yuen received a double punishment for stealing and lying.

I listened to Ah-yuen's story without surprise. I knew that my aunt was as cruel as my mother and that little could be done about it. Then I had an idea. 'Go inside and watch. Let's see if my aunt dares do anything to me,' I said.

My mother would not allow anyone to beat me other

than herself and Popo, and I knew she would be annoyed if my aunt laid a finger on me. She would consider she had lost face and would pounce on my aunt. I picked up the bamboo pole, hit the guava tree hard and brought down the ripe guavas with some unripe ones. Ah-yuen watched, wide-eyed with alarm, as I collected them in a basket and dragged it into the house to where Popo and my aunt were having tea.

'Popo,' I said, 'I picked them for the altar.'

Popo smiled approvingly. She liked to have ripe guava on the altar for its fragrance, but Aunt Chiew-foong's eyes nearly popped out. She stooped by the basket and ran her fingers over the fruit, then 'These are from my tree!' she screeched. 'Why did you pick so many?' She caught hold of my wrist and raised her hand but before she could hurt me, I said, 'If you hit me I will tell my mother, and she won't let you eat at our house.'

My aunt released me. 'If you want the fruit I will pick them for you in future,' she snapped.

From the corner of my eye I could see Ah-yuen concealing a smile with her hand.

Miew-kin and I were with Popo on one of her twice-monthly visits to the temple in Chinatown when she came across a cousin, Mrs Goh, with whom she had fallen out over a tontine investment. They had not spoken for a long time but that day, after prayers, they were sitting at the same table for the meal and began to talk to each other. Cousin Goh was grumbling about how hard it was to find a suitable bride for her son, Poh-chye, a manual worker. Also, she told Popo, they were too poor to use the services of a professional matchmaker and had little to offer as a dowry to the bride's family. 'But he's a good boy, always comes home straight after work, not like many of our young men who waste their money on gambling and smoking opium. He doesn't even go to prostitutes,' she said proudly.

She spoke loudly enough for everyone at the table to hear in the hope that a worshipper had a daughter who might marry her son. As Popo listened, a gleam came into her eye, and when we left the temple, we went to see Aunt Chiew-foong. Popo told her about the encounter with her estranged cousin who could not find a bride for her son, and how she had decided to match him with Ah-yuen. 'It's time to give the *muichai* her freedom. Make her presentable and I will arrange a meeting.'

My aunt was dumbfounded. It had never occurred to her that Ah-yuen might leave. 'I always thought she'd stay until the children are grown-up. You'll have to talk to my husband. I can't give permission,' she said.

'*Your* permission!' Popo was beside herself. 'Ah-yuen is *my* property. I made it clear to you in the beginning that I would decide when she should have her freedom. Your husband did not pay a cent for her.'

'She is a *muichai*, Ma. How can she marry?' said Aunt Chiew-foong, trying another tack.

'She will make Cousin Goh a good daughter-in-law,' Popo said.

At her next visit to the temple, Popo agreed a date with Cousin Goh for her and her son to meet Ah-yuen. If the girl seemed acceptable, they could talk about marriage. On the appointed day, Popo gave Ah-yuen a new cotton *samfoo* and explained why Cousin Goh and her son would visit later that day. Ah-yuen whispered to me that her prayers had been answered: she would be free at last. She understood now why my aunt had been so bad-tempered since Popo's last visit.

'The *muichai*'s visitors cannot use the front door,' my aunt had warned Popo, so when they arrived Popo brought Cousin Goh and her son through the garden to the back of the house and the kitchen. They sat at the table while Ah-yuen served them jasmine tea – she told me later that her hand had been shaking so much she could hardly pour it.

When Popo and I next visited my aunt, Ah-yuen whispered to me that she had been so excited at the prospect of freedom that food was no longer important. The gnawing hunger seemed to have vanished. Now when my aunt slapped her or knuckled her head, the pain was soon gone, thanks to her new-found happiness. 'Poh-chye has kind eyes, Miew-yong,' she confided. 'I want to have many children with him.'

Arrangements were made for Poh-chye and Ah-yuen to marry within three months. According to Popo, that would give my aunt time to find a servant to replace Ah-yuen. In the meantime, Poh-chye and his mother saw Ah-yuen a few times to talk about the marriage plans, and love blossomed between the pair. But Aunt Chiew-foong could not find a servant willing to undertake all the work in her house – a 'one-leg-kick', as they were known – for the wage she was offering. She faced the prospect of paying either for another *muichai*, or a living wage for one or two servants. What was more, she was expecting another baby. She told Popo that she had looked hard for a servant, but had failed to find anyone suitable.

'A one-leg-kick for the money you're offering?' Mother said, laughing, one day when my aunt was at our house.

'No one will want to take on all that work,' Popo chipped in, 'not even for double the wages you're offering, unless she has two pairs of hands.'

'In a few weeks my baby will be born,' my aunt whined, ignoring their remarks.

'Tell Cong to engage a *pue yuet*. I've never done without a professional for my confinements,' Mother told her.

My aunt looked at her uncertainly. Then she told them the truth. She had decided not to let Ah-yuen go and had put a stop to the wedding. 'We will not pay for a servant,' she said. 'If Ah-yuen were to marry, who would care for the children when the baby arrives? It is best for her to wait until she is older. There will always be other suitors.' Popo and Mother were aghast but Aunt Chiew-foong knew that Popo respected Uncle Cong so she made her next words sound like a threat. 'Ma, you know my husband is careful with money. If Ah-yuen leaves, he may be very angry.'

Now Popo was in a quandary. She had never before crossed swords with her second son-in-law. If it had been my father, she would not have hesitated but she did not have the courage to confront Cong. After some thought she told my aunt that for now she would postpone her plans.

The next day Cousin Goh arrived at our house, demanding to talk to Popo, and was reluctantly invited in. She said that Poh-chye had been to see Ah-yuen for a final discussion about the wedding but my aunt had stopped him at the gate. 'Ah-yuen doesn't want to see you,' she had said coldly.

'But – but our wedding is in a few days' time!' Poh-chye stammered.

'She can't go through with it but she is afraid to tell you so,' said my aunt. 'You are not her only . . . friend.'

My aunt had turned her back on Poh-chye and hurried into the house. Cousin Goh said her son had thought of approaching my uncle but hadn't the courage to talk to him because he was always so aloof with him. Poh-chye was bewildered, Cousin Goh went on. Ah-yuen had confessed her love for him and he was determined to find out why she had changed her mind. If there was another suitor, she stressed, they would understand and put aside her promise, but she must tell him so to his face: 'I will not be satisfied until I have seen Ah-yuen one last time and talked to her,' her son had said.

I watched Popo as she listened to all this, wondering how she would react. When Cousin Goh had finished speaking, Popo stood up and said that she was sorry but Ah-yuen must have changed her mind. There was nothing she could do about it as the *muichai* lived with her daughter and son-in-law. Then she hurried Poh-Chye's mother out of the door.

After that meeting, Popo avoided Cousin Goh: she went to the temple very early in the morning and left the rickshaw to wait while she burnt joss sticks and made her contribution. She was hoping that the matter would blow over. 'Given time, Poh-chye will find another girl,' she said, and put the episode out of her mind.

Then a letter arrived from Cousin Goh. Her son was behaving strangely: he had stopped going to work and stayed locked in his room all day. Sometimes she could hear him crying and talking to himself. He had tried to see Ah-yuen several times but my aunt had threatened to send for the police if he returned again. Once, he had waited in the field behind the house, hoping to catch Ah-yuen hanging out the laundry, but to no avail. Finally he had tried to speak to Popo: he was too shy to come to the house but he had felt sure he would bump into her at the temple . . . 'Please come urgently and talk to him,' Cousin Goh ended. Her letter was ignored.

That afternoon we visited Aunt Chiew-foong and I saw Ah-yuen again. She told me that when Poh-chye had first been sent away, she had been locked in the bathroom under orders to keep quiet or face a severe beating. 'But I know he loves me, and will find a way to set me free.' Every day, when she had finished the housework she went to the altar in the hall, where my pious aunt prayed, lit joss sticks and knelt before the statue of Kuan Yin, the goddess of mercy and protector of women.

The next day Popo received a message that Poh-chye had been found hanging from a beam in his room. In spite of the tragedy, neither Popo nor Aunt Chiew-foong told Ah-yuen that he had committed suicide.

Soon after Poh-chye's funeral, Popo was outraged to learn that Mrs Goh was at my aunt's house. 'She has no right to go to Chiew-foong's house and blame her for Poh-chye's suicide,' she fumed. She changed into her silk clothes, which she always wore when she went out, and left for my aunt's house, muttering imprecations to herself. As I watched her disappear down the road, I heard her shouting at the rickshaw-puller to run faster.

Popo was with her *chimui* a few days later when someone said that Ah-yuen had left my aunt's house. I wondered why Aunt Chiew-foong had let her go now, after all that had happened, but when my aunt next visited no one mentioned Ah-yuen.

On my way home from an errand a few months later, I came across a group of novice nuns. Their heads were shaven and they wore long grey tunics that covered them to their ankles, trousers, black cotton shoes and a string of prayer beads. They were walking silently with their heads bowed. I glanced at them, then stared at a familiar face among them. I walked towards them still trying to work out who the face belonged to, when it struck me. Of course! It was Ah-yuen. When I had last seen her she had had shiny black hair in two plaits down to her waist. As I passed her, she did not acknowledge me. I stopped to watch them walk on and remembered the sweetness of Ah-yuen's nature. Despite the beatings and starvation, she had loved my aunt's children. And she was brave: her spirit had been intact after all she had suffered and she had never given up hope of freedom and children of her own. Now she had been destroyed by my aunt's selfishness. I wanted to tell her I was ashamed that Chiew-foong was my aunt.

I followed the novices and saw them turn into a lane near Orchard Road, and enter a house surrounded by a wall. I stood looking up at the tops of the star-fruit trees that grew behind it and wondered how to get in. A branch overhung the wall and I saw that I could use it to help me climb over it.

When I dropped down on the other side, I almost landed on a novice who was tending the garden. 'I must see Ah-yuen,' I gasped. She listened to my story, then told me to wait while she tried to find her.

At last Ah-yuen arrived. 'Go away before you get me into trouble, Miew-yong,' she said, but I pulled her behind a bush, out of sight, and we began to talk. After Poh-chye's funeral, Ah-yuen said, his mother had come to see her, convinced that her son would still have been alive if Ah-yuen had not rejected him. She was determined to find out why she had changed her mind. 'That morning,' Ah-yuen went on, 'I was in the kitchen, washing clothes. Your aunt was playing with the children so no one heard the gate opening and Mrs Goh came through the garden to the back of the house and found me.' She had thought that Poh-chye's mother had come to tell her the wedding was to take place after all, so she greeted her with a smile.

'How can you smile when my son is not yet cold in his grave? You should be ashamed of yourself!'

Ah-yuen froze. 'What are you talking about?' Then she burst into tears and sobbed inconsolably. When she could speak again, she said, 'If Poh-chye is dead, I want to die too, rather than live without him. I can't stay a *muichai* all my life. I'll hang myself, like he did.'

As she said this, Aunt Chiew-foong appeared at the door. 'You can't hang yourself here!' she shrieked. 'I don't want my house to be haunted.' It was then that she had run to the rickshaw stand to summon Popo.

When Popo arrived Ah-yuen and Cousin Goh were sitting on low wooden stools in the garden, heads bowed. Popo had immediately let rip, but before she could finish, Cousin Goh had raised her head and pointed a finger at her. 'You and your daughter Chiew-foong are black-hearted people with no regard for others. You might as well have killed my son with your bare hands. But for you, he would still be alive.'

Popo could think of no response to this and left them alone. Mrs Goh took Ah-yuen's hand and talked to her gently, eventually persuading her not to harm herself. 'One death is enough,' she concluded.

Ah-yuen agreed. 'Poh-chye was my first and only love,' she said. 'I will never marry anyone else. Instead I shall become a nun. Will you help me?'

That day she left my aunt's house to stay with Cousin Goh, and soon afterwards entered a temple of Kuan Yin as a novice.

It was a sad, sad story, but now, Ah-yuen said, she was

happy. I said goodbye, and watched her walk back towards the temple.

When I got home I took Ah-pin outside, where we would not be overheard, and told her what I had found out. She started to cry, but she was glad that her cousin was alive.

A month had passed since Andrew had assaulted Ah-pin and my mother and Popo were still trying to decide what to do with her. Andrew was a government servant with a forthcoming inheritance from his grandfather so he, of course, could not have been at fault, which meant that Ah-pin had 'disgraced' our household. They decided to sell her to another family. Andrew would be mollified and they would make a tidy profit. They put the word out among Mother's *mah-jongg* circle and Popo's *chimui*.

My mother found a family interested in purchasing a *muichai* but, first, they wanted to look her over. When the lady of the house saw Ah-pin, she rejected her straight away: such a beautiful, shapely girl would tempt her husband. Time and again Ah-pin was turned down, but Popo was determined to dispose of her. She contacted some friends who had connections with the *tongs* in the gambling dens. One morning, I heard a struggle and someone screaming. I ran out of the bathroom to see Ah-pin being dragged out of the front door by two strangers. Popo had sold her to a brothel.

Twenty-one

In the last year of the occupation people took biscuit tins filled with money to the shops to buy food because inflation was rising so fast that the Japanese currency was almost worthless. Popo was finding it hard to make ends meet, and finally relinquished her grip on the family's purse strings. Mother took over, and stopped giving free meals to all the so-called friends and hangers-on who had taken advantage of Popo's hospitality. Gradually, when they realized that Chinese tea was all they would get when they came to our house, they stopped visiting. But Aunt Chiew-foong continued to bring her children to eat with us three times a week.

One evening they got up and left quickly after dinner, as usual, but my father spotted my aunt doubling back through the garden and making her way furtively to the kitchen door, where Popo handed her a jute sack. He left the house, grabbed the sack and held it upside down. Several cans of food landed on the ground. Popo held the key to the storeroom that contained our emergency supplies, and he had never asked her how much she had used. Now she had betrayed his trust. He was furious.

My aunt blamed Popo: 'I didn't ask for it. She forced it all on me.' She kicked the cans.

Popo turned on Father. 'Have you forgotten that you

have no rights in this household? But for me, where would you have been when your mother died? I shall give my daughter what she needs.'

My mother had heard Popo scolding Father and came out, intending to take her side, but when she discovered that the argument was about the theft of our provisions she was angry with her mother and sister and joined in the fracas. The noise was unbearable – all three women were screaming at each other.

'I feel sorry for her,' Popo said to Mother, 'and I wanted to give her enough so that she can stop coming here.' She added, 'It is degrading that she has to depend on *him* for survival.' It was an unkind reference to my father.

I had often seen Popo put a sack by the kitchen door for my aunt, but had never said anything for fear of the lighted wick. Now that my mother had found out about the dealings between Popo and her sister she was upset as well as angry. She had allowed Popo to live with us and rule the household, which had given Popo status among her friends at the temple. Mother had always thought she was closest to Popo, but this illusion had been shattered by her mother's deceit. From now on when Popo went to visit my aunt, Mother insisted on inspecting the contents of her basket to make sure she was taking nothing but fruit and eggs. Afterwards, Popo would not speak to her for a day or two.

Everything was expensive, including fuel for cooking. Before the occupation we had had enough charcoal under the stove to cook three meals a day and to make the weekly quantity of herbal potions and bird's-nest soup. Now we could afford to buy enough fuel for just one hot meal every day. The next day we reheated the leftovers from dinner for lunch, and used the firewood sparingly.

Our Japanese neighbours stored their logs in the garage they had taken from us and had fixed a large padlock to the door, which scraped and crunched on the ground when it opened. When I heard that noise, I would run to the window to see what was going on. It was invariably the gardener with his wheelbarrow, collecting firewood to take into the neighbours' house. When the pile dwindled, a lorry would arrive at our drive, usually with an armed Japanese soldier in front with the driver. They would reverse up to the garage and unload the wood. When the driver was alone and no one was in sight, Popo would pay him to leave enough for a few weeks under the bushes in our garden.

One night, just before bedtime, Beng ran into the kitchen and told Popo he had seen children from the *kampung* carrying a ladder and making their way to the back of the garage. He wanted her to go with him and investigate. Uninvited, I followed. It was a little while before our eyes had adjusted to the dark but eventually we were astonished to see the children stealing firewood. Logs were being poked through a gap between the wall and the roof of the garage and the child at the top of the ladder passed them down to the others. A boy saw us approaching, whistled softly, and a small girl squeezed out through the gap near the roof. Caught stealing from the Japanese, the frightened children crowded round Popo. *'Nonya, tolong, jangan bilang,'* one whispered, pleading with Popo not to inform on them. Another suggested that Beng should join them if we wanted some wood, and waited anxiously for his reply.

I was amazed at the children's daring and wondered if their parents had sent them to steal the wood. I could see that Popo was thinking the same thing: she was peering uncertainly at the shadows by the bushes, trying to see if anyone was hiding there to watch what was happening. If she reported the theft she would make enemies among the Malay families. In any case, it was common knowledge that the Japanese looked upon the Malays as their friends, and exposing their children might backfire – they might say we were the thieves. Eventually Popo said she would tell no one and added, 'Beng will join you tomorrow night.' Later, she justified her decision to Mother: 'Those Japanese devils stole the car, which I paid for with my tontine money, and the firewood is stored in our garage. There is nothing wrong with taking something back.'

The next evening, my mother fussed over Beng as she prepared him for the robbery. She made him wear a long-sleeved shirt and long trousers, then gave him a pair of Father's socks, and told him to put them on his hands. 'To protect your hands from splinters,' she said tenderly, as she pulled them up his arms and secured them with rubber bands.

When he was ready, he looked like a scarecrow. 'I'm afraid of the centipedes that like to hide in the logs!' he cried, and burst into tears. 'I saw Mother tread on one with her clogs. Don't make me go.' He continued to cry until Popo relented. She looked at me and said, 'You can go instead.'

Beng stopped sobbing and smiled.

'No!' I protested. 'I'm scared of the centipedes too.'

Popo threatened to tell my mother, who was in her bedroom, that I wouldn't do as I was told, and I changed my mind. I'd rather put up with centipedes than one of my mother's beatings. That night, I stood on the ladder passing logs down the line of children. They were heavy, but after several trips, carrying two at a time in the dark, I had brought my share home. The centipedes had left me alone and so had the other insects, and I decided Beng had been silly to make such a fuss.

The pile of twelve logs did not impress Popo: 'We can have soup,' she said, but uttered not a word of thanks.

Bird's-nest soup was at the top of Popo's list of healthy foods. In fact, she believed that any type of foodstuff had health-improving properties if it was prepared in the right way by those who knew about such things. She prided herself on her expertise and was full of tips such as, 'Steaming food for several hours is best for healing fatigue and it will also help keep the body healthy,' and 'Herbal soups and medicines should be boiled for one to three hours depending on the type of herbs.' She said that the nests she used for her soup were made from the saliva of Asian swifts. After the wedges of nest had been soaked for a few hours, Yan-fok, Miew-kin and I sat at the kitchen table with our tweezers picking out the feathers. The more expensive nests had fewer but Popo bought the cheaper ones. Sometimes she steamed them in a tureen with strips of chicken, but more often with rock sugar, which was how Beng preferred it.

The firewood stealing went on for weeks, and we had enough fuel now to cook two meals a day. I knew my father wouldn't approve and worried that he would get into trouble if I was caught, so I decided to stop. The next time the children knocked and asked if I wanted to join them, I said no. As I closed the door, Popo appeared. 'How can you refuse an opportunity to save money for the family?' she asked, twisting my ear. So I went out after them. When I got to the garage, the ladder was already in place, leaning against the wall. The tallest boy said to me, 'Tonight it's your turn to climb in and pass the logs out. We've all done it.'

I wanted to tell him that he was too fat to fit through the gap but decided it was not the time to pick a fight. There wasn't much space between the top of the wall and the roof but I put my leg through the opening and squeezed in. My skirt caught on a nail and the sound of the cloth tearing seemed so loud in the quiet night and the Japanese officers were just yards away. We could not risk using a candle, and as I peered into inky darkness, I felt as if I was being shut into a box. I began to pass out the wood, promising myself this would be the last time, no matter what threats Popo came up with.

'Make sure you only move the top ones,' someone said. 'If you take too many from the same place you'll get hurt if the rest roll down on you.'

Eventually I was climbing unsteadily down the ladder, glad to be in the outside world again. The other children left my share of the logs on the ground and disappeared back to their *kampung*. I piled the wood outside the kitchen door and sat on the steps to catch my breath. Popo appeared, knuckled my head and whispered, 'Bring the wood inside and stack it under the stove.'

'I'm tired. Can't Beng do it?' I said.

But Popo knew how to make me do as she wanted. 'If our neighbours see that wood, they'll know where it came from. Your father will be in trouble with the Japanese devils.'

After I had stacked the last log under the stove, I realized that every exposed part of my body stung. Splinters were lodged under my fingernails, in my hands, arms and legs. I'd been too frightened of getting caught to feel the pain until now. I went into the dining room, turned on the light, found a pair of tweezers in the sewing box and began to pull out the splinters. When I squealed with pain, Popo rushed in. 'Be quiet! You'll wake your father! He mustn't find out you took the firewood,' she said.

'But you told me to,' I muttered, as she pulled me into Dai-chay's old room.

Ever since Dai-chay had died there, the room had been used only for storing broken furniture until it was repaired. Mother, Popo and the other servants avoided it after dusk when they believed the spirits of the dead roamed. They were sure that Dai-chay haunted the room so it had become my refuge. The only company I had there were the mice that had taken over the tall cabinet that contained a broken gramophone. They had given birth to their young there and I sometimes amused myself with the blind, hairless baby mice, picking them up by their tails and gently swinging them about. I sat on the bed and went on removing splinters. When I was too tired to go on, I tiptoed into our darkened bedroom, trying not to disturb anyone.

Popo turned on her bedside lamp. 'You can't go to bed yet. You haven't washed,' she said.

When I came out of the bathroom she was beside the door. 'Show me your hands and feet.' It was very late, but Popo would not waive the rule. Then she noticed that one of my gold earrings was missing. 'You must have lost it in the garage. You'll go back and find it tomorrow night.'

I was tired and sore and I couldn't have cared less about my earring. For once, I dared to answer her back. 'I won't go back ever, and if you try to make me I'll tell Father,' I said.

Popo swore, but she didn't want to raise her voice at half past midnight so I won that battle.

That night might have been the last time I stole fire-wood from the Japanese, but Popo soon found another job for me. Rice or sugar were sometimes available, rationed, and distributed from a building near the mosque behind my house. A large queue would form the night before it was to be given out and the police recruited marshals from the relatives of those who worked at the station to stop people jumping the queue. Each marshal was paid in rice for the day's work, and my father suggested that Beng could do it for a day.

'But he will fall ill standing in the sun,' Popo said.

Once again, I was sent in Beng's place but this time I did not mind: I enjoyed helping to keep people in line and earning my share of the rice.

One day I got home to discover that misfortune had befallen the chicken farmer who had sheltered us during the first days of the bombing. He knew some people who worked at a club for the Japanese and often bought stolen food from them to sell on the black-market. One morning, he had bought a few katties of rice and some sugar from one of the chefs. On the way home he was stopped at a roadblock and searched. Unable to explain where the food had come from, he was taken to the police station. That evening, when Father got home he told us what had happened. At first, the farmer had tried not to get anyone else into trouble, but after a severe beating he had told the interrogator that he had bought the food from a chef at the Japanese club. Later that day, my father was passing the cells when the farmer called to him. His face was so swollen that it took Father a moment to recognize him. The man had helped us and asked nothing in return – he was a good friend, and my father was determined to help him. He listened to his story, then set off to see the restaurant manager at the Japanese club, a fellow Hainanese called Lim Kah-heng.

When he walked into the club's grounds he could not see the main building, a former Chinese school, as it was screened by tall hibiscus hedges and the garden was ablaze with scarlet, mauve and pink bougainvilleas. At the far end, Japanese soldiers relaxed beneath palm trees as waiters served them drinks. In the club restaurant, he could see Japanese soldiers and civilians being waited on by women in *cheongsam*, sarong *kebaya* or kimonos. He made his way to the side of the building where one of the chefs showed him into Lim's office. Lim was in his late twenties, slim, wearing a suit and bow tie. He smiled and stood up to shake hands. He was tall by Chinese standards, more than six feet, rather dashing and handsome.

Before Father could speak, Lim said, defensively, 'You're from the police station. Is anything the matter?' Plainly he thought that he was in trouble. Quickly Father explained, in their native dialect, the reason for his visit and told Lim of how the farmer had sheltered us during the dangerous days of the invasion and of his concern now for the man's life. By now Lim had relaxed and was prepared to help, although he claimed to know nothing about the stolen food. 'I'll sort it out,' he said. 'I'll get the Japanese officer in charge of the club to clear the man and have him released,' he promised.

Father thanked him and got ready to leave – he wanted to tell the farmer the good news – but Lim went on talking. From time to time, beautifully dressed women popped into the office with complaints or requests. 'They're always squabbling among themselves,' Lim said. 'They tell me everything.' He winked. 'If you're interested, we have rooms upstairs . . .'

Despite the lewd parting shot, Lim was true to his word and the farmer was freed. In time, he and my father became friends and he often came to see us. Sometimes he would arrive with food and cook a meal for us. At other times he appeared with his elder brother and played *mah-jongg* with Popo and Mother.

It was soon after Lim and Father became friends that I stopped going to the Malay school. Every month or so, mother would trim our hair, using her sewing scissors. It was on one such occasion that she found lice and nits in mine, which threw the household into a panic. First, it was considered dirty but, more importantly, it meant bad luck to my superstitious family. I had to stay in the garden while the whole house was turned upside down, and my bedding was burnt in the garden. Everyone's hair was checked, even the servants', but no one else had them. My mother decided to shave my head.

I was appalled. 'How can I go to school or do the shopping with a bald head?' I asked. 'Everyone will laugh at me.'

'Hah!' my mother said, and went for Father's razor.

'You can beat me to death, but I won't go to school or do the shopping if you shave my head,' I said.

She ignored me, but I pleaded with her to leave two inches. 'I'll do anything you want if you'll just leave me some hair.'

I didn't know how I had picked up the lice but my mother was convinced they'd come from the Malay children. 'You're the only one in the family who makes friends with them,' she said.

I wasn't allowed to go back to the Malay school and was forbidden to see my friends from the *kampung*. Every day for a week after Mother had found the lice, Popo sat me on a low stool in the bathroom and poured neat Jeyes fluid over my head. It burnt my skin but I had to keep still while she used a fine-tooth comb to remove the pests from my hair. Everyone in the family, except my father, kept away from me, so I spent a lot of time in Dai-chay's old room with the mice or sat under the jackfruit tree in the garden playing with the ants. I missed my friends and I was bored, so I was pleased when a trishaw stopped outside our house one wet Sunday afternoon. Lim stepped out into the rain and opened a waxed paper umbrella over a pretty young woman. I thought she must be Miss Shang, a hostess from the Japanese club. Popo had prescribed a few herbal remedies for Lim and I had heard him ask if he could bring Miss Shang to see her: she had a rash on her leg.

Miss Shang was stunning: slim and elegant, she was much younger than my mother, with an oval face and long glossy black hair that flowed down her back. She was wearing a pale green ankle-length *cheongsam* trimmed with dark green piping and decorated with a dragon embroidered in dark green and gold, with a pair of gold shoes. I followed them inside and noticed that, in spite of the five-inch stiletto heels, she walked gracefully into the sitting room, where Popo and Mother were talking. Mother looked at Lim, then at Miss Shang. Without a word, she got up and left the room. Such bad manners were unheard of before outsiders, and it was clear that Lim and Miss Shang were discomfited.

'Pumpkin-seed face,' Popo said, with a smile, and inclined her head to Miss Shang. It was a quiet compliment, and Miss Shang was disarmed. She smiled back.

When she lifted her *cheongsam* to show Popo the inflammation, her legs were smooth and hairless. Popo had told us that girls who shaved their legs became scared of the dark and we had never pulled so much as a single hair out of our legs. I wondered if Miss Shang had heard this saying. After Popo had inspected her legs, Miss Shang helped her carry the remedy ingredients into the kitchen, then walked about opening cupboards and drawers to find the utensils Popo needed.

Some weeks later, when Mother happened to be out, she returned to tell Popo that the rash had cleared up and handed her a bag of glutinous rice flour, with some other ingredients, to make sweet dumplings. This time she was wearing a red *cheongsam* with chrysanthemum flowers embroidered in black sequins. Popo hadn't forgotten Mother's behaviour on Miss Shang's previous visit, and was curious to know whether there was anything between Miss Shang and Lim. She pretended to be concerned about the lifestyle that might have brought about Miss Shang's rash, then asked the questions to which she really wanted answers.

'Me and Lim?' Miss Shang laughed. 'He has no money and he's only a restaurant manager. What can he offer me?'

Recently my mother had become even more short-tempered and took it out on Miew-kin, our remaining *muichai* Yan-fok, and me. One evening after dinner, Yan-fok was carrying a heavy tureen, used for steaming bird's-nest soup, to the kitchen when she slipped and fell. The tureen was smashed. Yan-fok knew it was valuable – she had been told several times to be careful with it – and cringed with terror. 'It was an accident – don't hit me,' she begged. But my mother flung back her chair, with such force that it crashed to the floor, ran to Yan-fok, grabbed a handful of her hair and slapped her. Yan-fok covered her face with her hands as Mother sat on her stomach and banged her head against the cement floor. Yan-fok could not move but she screamed.

Popo lit her after-dinner cigarette coolly and watched. My father, in a vest and shorts, left the room to get dressed and go out. He knew that my mother would only stop when she was exhausted. But Miew-kin and I, terrified that Mother would crack Yan-fok's skull, rushed forward to try to stop her. I pulled at her arms while Miew-kin put her hands under Yan-fok's head to cushion it against the floor. Mother was stunned. She glared at us, then got up. She left Yan-fok on the floor and forced Miew-kin down, sat on her, grasped her hair and began to bang her head against the floor. When I tried to pull Mother off her, she turned on me, but she was tired and I fought so hard that she gave up.

I had hated touching my mother since I was very young. One day when she was having a nap I had stroked her arm. She had woken and hit me because I had disturbed her. Now, even in a rickshaw, I would do my utmost to avoid her.

Yan-fok never recovered from that beating, and Mother complained that she had become simple-minded and stubborn. She was almost deaf, her speech was slurred and she found it difficult to understand what was said to her. Mother and Popo tried to cure her with a knuckle to her head when they thought she was neglecting her duties, but Miew-kin and I wondered what would become of her.

Twenty-two

Every year on the fifth day of the fifth lunar month at the time of the Dragon Boat Festival Popo's eyes were red with crying. Miew-kin, Wang-lai and I were puzzled by her sadness, but never brave enough to ask her or Mother to explain. Despite the wartime shortages, most Chinese bought the celebratory *chong* ready-made in Chinatown because it was difficult to prepare, but Popo was an expert. As she got out the ingredients, sniffing and red-eyed, Beng said to Mother, 'If you don't tell me why she's crying, I'll ask her.'

Mother took him into the garden and I followed – I was desperate to hear the answer. For once, she did not seem to mind that I was there. 'I would have had a brother today if things had gone differently for Popo,' Mother told Beng. 'Her heart was broken and so was Kung-kung's. He wanted his first-born to be a son. Popo was expecting her first baby, which was long overdue. The village midwife was worried because the water bag inside Popo had burst many hours earlier and there was no kicking from the baby inside her womb. She broke a piece off a ceramic bowl to make a sharp knife, boiled it to make it clean, then twisted a length of cloth for Popo to bite on and cut her so that she could pull the baby out. But it was too late. Her son was born dead on the day of the Dragon Boat Festival and she has never got over it.'

We went back inside, and Mother coaxed Popo into making *chong* to distract her. My grandmother took a long, wide dried leaf and softened it in hot water. Then she made a fold half-way along it, twisted it into a cone, half filled it with glutinous rice and cooked meat, then folded the leaf into a pyramid. When she had finished she tied it with string. Mother had never mastered the art of tying *chong* securely, so that the rice would not leak during cooking, so she was left to tie the pyramids into bunches of ten and put them to boil for three hours.

By July, we had spent three and a half years under Japanese rule. One day when my father seemed even more anxious and miserable than usual I asked him how things were at work. He sighed. The Japanese favoured Malay and Indian workers over the Chinese, who were persecuted and often killed. Until the occupation most Malays had taken minor posts in the government service but since the Japanese had been in charge, that had changed. They resented taking orders from a Chinese. Also, the Japanese had become nervous and erratic, which Father suspected was linked to setbacks in the war. Lots of people were talking about a 'turning-point' and he knew, from conversations he had overheard between Japanese officers, that in May the Germans had surrendered. The atmosphere in his office was strained and Lye, his assistant, still bore him a grudge for not allowing him to move in with us.

At home Father had no peace because Popo's *chimui* were constantly dropping in, while he and Mother were at daggers drawn. He was in despair and found consolation only in drink. People had died after too much *samsu*, yet he went on drinking at night in his office.

However, he would soon be taking his annual holiday, and planned to spend a few days fishing off the Jurong coast. He loved the seaside and would often cycle there to watch the sunrise and buy crabs or large black prawns from a fisherman, coming in with his night's catch in a small, narrow rowing-boat, called a *kolek*. 'The best way to eat seafood is to cook it on the beach, fresh, in seawater,' he would say. Kim-teck, a friend, and his sons were to go with him and Beng on the trip. The two men had served together in civil defence during the bombing raids. Kim-teck had a four-bedroom bungalow in Dunearn Road, and while Father played *mah-jongg* with him, I would go for long walks with his daughter, Rosie.

Early on the morning of 19 July, Father and Beng were getting ready to go. Beng couldn't contain his excitement: it was his first fishing trip and he had checked and rechecked his tackle. 'Papa, we haven't any worms,' he said.

Father was busy and didn't answer so Beng asked again. Finally Father snapped, 'Don't bother me now. We can pick up anything we need when we get there.'

Yesterday Father had spotted Beng hiding among the banana trees in our front garden to smoke, so engrossed in it that he didn't notice Father run into the garden. It was one of the rare times that he had disciplined Beng without my mother or Popo's intervention. Now, despite the fishing trip, he was still annoyed.

Everything was packed and they were ready to leave, when Popo cried, 'My left eye! Something bad always happens when it twitches.' She grabbed Beng's hand. 'He's never been fishing before. He mustn't go near water – it's dangerous.'

'But I want to go fishing! Let me go, Popo!' Beng pleaded.

'We must heed premonitions. Bad things happen to those who ignore them,' she said.

Beng began to cry. At that moment, Father walked in from pumping up the bicycle tyres. He pulled my brother away from Popo. 'What's the matter now?' he barked.

'Don't blame Beng,' Popo said, a little taken aback. 'My premonition came from the gods.'

'What premonition is this, then?' He was in no mood to listen. He picked up his luggage and flung it across the room, missing her by inches. 'A pretext to stop me going, I suppose. As usual.' With that he stormed out of the house.

It was not until late in the afternoon that he came home. He went straight to bed without putting on his pyjamas. A few minutes later he called for a spittoon and vomited. We thought he had drunk too much so we weren't worried and Popo said we should let him sleep it off. At dinnertime, though, we couldn't wake him. My brothers, sisters and I stood at the foot of the bed, while Popo and Mother shook him and called his name. Blood trickled out of his mouth.

Sum-chay, who was standing beside him, shouted, 'Quick! Fetch smelling-salts.'

But there were no smelling-salts or any other Western medicines in the house. Popo continued to shake him.

Sum-chay turned to me. 'Why are you still here?' she asked.

I looked at her blankly. I had no idea what she meant. 'I'll go to the upstairs flat and ask if they have smelling-salts,' I said.

'There's no time for that,' she replied.

In Cantonese smelling-salts are called *mah-neu*, or horse's urine, and Popo believed any urine could be used in place of the salts because both contain ammonia. 'A substitute is better than nothing,' she said, and went to the kitchen. She returned with a cup, made Sai-ngau urinate into it, then held it under my father's nose. At that moment our Malay neighbour upstairs, attracted by the commotion, rushed down. 'Maybe it's a spell. Send for a *bomoh* to cast it out,' he suggested. My mother agreed, so the man left and returned a little later with an elderly bespectacled Malay woman. We children were sent out of the room and Mother shut the door.

After fifteen minutes, the *bomoh* emerged from the bedroom with a dinner plate on which lay a piece of broken glass on some bloodstained cotton wool. 'Someone had put a spell on him but I have removed it,' she said proudly.

After she had gone we were allowed back into the bedroom and I stood beside Father willing him to sit up and open his eyes. He did not move and blood continued to seep from his mouth. Then he went into convulsions. When they ceased and he was still, blood continued to dribble from his mouth. An hour later it stopped. His body was limp, his eyes closed. Popo took Wang-lai and Sai-ngau out of the room.

After they had gone I studied my father's face. It was peaceful, as though he had fallen into a deep sleep. He no longer looked old and dejected. I touched his feet and left the room. As I closed the door I heard Mother and Popo arguing in the dining room. They seldom quarrelled, but now their voices were raised.

'Poh-mun was baptized a Methodist when he attended the Anglo-Chinese School. It would be wrong to disregard his religion. We will have to get in touch with a pastor,' Mother said.

'His religion is not important now,' Popo said. 'I will arrange a Chinese funeral for him.'

I was confused. Why were they talking about funerals and Father's religion? Our family, including Father, went to the Chinese temple and burned joss sticks at home. Then I remembered that Father had once hung a picture of Jesus Christ in his bedroom and called us children to kneel with him in prayer. Popo had burst into the room, stopped the prayers and removed the picture.

That evening my father was laid on a makeshift bed of wooden planks in the sitting room, facing the front door. My mother lit joss sticks and an oil lamp, and placed them by his side. Late that night when everyone was asleep, I got up and went into the sitting room. I stood and stared at Father for a long time. Then I unrolled a mat on the floor next to him, lay down and slept, so that I would be there when he woke in the morning.

At dawn I got up, unbolted the door and went out into the Muslim cemetery. I pushed into the thick undergrowth, through the tall bracken towards the mango trees and the chameleons. Popo loathed reptiles, I remembered.

When I arrived at the clearing, I leant against a mango tree and looked up into its spreading branches, which filtered the early-morning sunlight on to my face. I realized I had to face the truth. Father was dead and the light had gone out of my life. I dropped to the ground and sat there for hours, thinking about him. I thought about how hard he had worked to take care of his family, how kind he was, even though his wife and mother-in-law tormented him mercilessly. He had always made time to explain things calmly to me, never shouted and never hit me. He had tried, too, to follow the teachings of Confucius, which he had learnt from his mother on the farm where the rambutans and scarlet mangosteens grew. I remembered how, just a few weeks ago, I had been waiting to walk home with him when he had emerged from the police station with a short fat man. 'This is your grandfather,' he had said, and introduced me to Fat Lum, the stepfather who had stolen his inheritance.

During the days before the funeral visitors came to pay their respects, bringing gifts of white gold, *pak kum*, which was the custom unless the bereaved family was very rich. Many of Father's old schoolfriends appeared, and talked about the camping and swimming trips of their boyhood. They knew that my father had been a Methodist and were surprised to see the joss sticks and the oil lamp beside his body. As some were Christians, they asked my mother if he had renounced his religion. She told them he had not, but that the household observed only the Taoist religion. They protested that he should be buried according to the rites of his faith and went to fetch the Methodist pastor. Mother told the clergyman to talk to Popo.

'Christianity has never been practised in this household,' Popo said grimly, as she placed more joss sticks beside Father's body, 'and this is a family matter. It has nothing to do with outsiders.'

But the pastor refused to back down. Popo flew into a rage but he was not intimidated, and when Father's friends backed him up, she agreed ungraciously to do as he wanted.

On the day of the funeral, Mother put on a display of grief. I had seldom seen her show any affection for Father when he was alive but now she wept and clung to the coffin as it was loaded on to the hearse, yelling, 'I won't let you go! I won't let you go!' At the burial ground she wailed and tore at her hair, and made as if to throw herself on to the coffin after it had been lowered into the ground.

My father was buried at the Bidadari cemetery in Serangoon Road, Singapore. Many years later, when the government wanted the land for development, his body was exhumed and cremated, the ashes placed in the columbarium.

Twenty-three

Lye had taken over Father's job at the police station. He had not forgotten that Father had refused to let him and his family move in with us and the day after the funeral he was on our doorstep armed with an order from the Japanese that gave us a week's notice to leave our home. 'This is my house now,' he said triumphantly, waving the document in my mother's face. 'Don't ask for sympathy – your husband showed none to me. If you and your family are not out in a week, I'll throw your belongings out on to the road.'

We had nowhere to go and we knew that Lye had meant what he'd said. We were in mourning, wearing black, so we couldn't visit the homes of friends or relatives to ask for help, or receive them at our house until a hundred days had passed. Until then, it was feared that the spirit of the dead still lingered and would bring bad luck. Popo sent a message to Aunt Chiew-foong, telling her that we had to move, and we expected her to worry about Popo and make room in her house for us, but two days before we had to leave, there was no sign of her.

In desperation Popo suggested her flat in Chinatown. 'Eight of us cannot fit into one room,' Mother said, 'and I want a room to myself.'

Two of Father's Muslim schoolfriends had been at his

funeral and now Mother remembered that they had said, 'If you are ever in need, we will always help the family of our good friend.' So, with no one else to turn to, she approached them. They owned many houses on the island and were appalled to hear how Lye had behaved. They promptly offered us a house at a low rent. It was large, with five bedrooms, three garages and quarters for two servants in Anderson Road, an exclusive area not far from the botanical gardens.

When my mother returned with the news, Miew-kin and I set off to look at the house, which was built on the side of a hill. Without a key we could only see the outside and through the windows, but it was beautiful. The branches of tall old trees spread like an umbrella over much of the garden, providing shade in the heat of the day, and for the first time since Father's death our hearts lifted.

When we returned home we found Mother and Lim in the sitting room, deep in conversation. We were not allowed to interrupt Popo or Mother when they had visitors so we suppressed our eagerness to tell Mother we loved the house, went into the bedroom and started to pack our things.

Since Lim had visited us with the beautiful Miss Shang, I had noticed a change in my mother's attitude towards him. Now when I heard her say goodbye to him I knew she was in a good mood so I went to tell her about the new house. She listened absently as I described the garden and the trees and said how much I was looking forward to living there.

'We are not taking the house in Anderson Road,' she said. 'It's too big. I've exchanged it for a smaller one in Orchard Road.'

I was disappointed, and puzzled. It wasn't until much later that I found out she was in love with Lim, and had been so even while my father was still alive, and had been telling him about the house on the day I had found them together. Lim was a heavy gambler, with many debts, and saw a chance to make money. He had a business friend who lived in a terraced house with his wife, two concubines and many children. It was too small for them all so he was on the lookout for a bigger property with a garden. He was also prepared to pay a large sum for the right house. When my mother told Lim about the house in Anderson Road he coaxed her into persuading our Muslim benefactors to let the house to his friend on the pretext that she preferred to live nearer to the shops in his friend's house. The exchange took place, and Lim pocketed his money.

Many of Father's friends from the police station helped us move. Much of the furniture belonged to the house, so we had little to take with us, except the wardrobe with the secret compartment, three double beds, a few pieces made of carved rosewood, household and personal things, my father's books, our clothes and the items from Popo's altar. When everything had been loaded on to the lorry, I felt sad. I was leaving the home where I could still feel my father's presence and the special places where I had spent many happy hours with Fatimah and my friends from the *kampung*. I knew I would miss it all.

Number 402 Orchard Road stood beside an open monsoon drain, about seven feet wide and five feet deep, which separated the pavement from the road. At one end of the row of houses there was a large coffee shop and several stalls offering a variety of food, including Indian curry, with *dosai* and *paratha*, Indonesian delicacies, and stuffed bean curd. A few doors away the grocer acted as an agent for the *chap-ji-kee* two-digit lottery. I had delivered the daily stake to this shop when the servants were too busy since I was seven. Popo didn't want to miss a single draw. If she did and her numbers came up, I faced a severe beating. It was too dangerous to cross the monsoon drain when it was flooded so at those times I would call to the shopkeeper and wait for him to collect the stake from me.

The sitting room, dining room and a long narrow kitchen were on the ground floor of our new house. Popo decided to put her double bed in the dining room because she did not like climbing stairs. Her legs were thin and weak and constantly needed massaging. She would often sit on her bed and point to her knee, lamenting, 'The knee is bigger than the thigh when you are going to die.' When she was asleep, we had to tiptoe about the house so that we didn't wake her. My mother chose the larger of the two bedrooms on the first floor for herself, and my brothers had the smaller one at the back. A flight of almost vertical steps led to a trapdoor that opened into a loft without windows or skylight and this was where Wang-lai, Yan-fok, Miew-kin and I slept, on the floorboards. Sum-chay had decided to retire and returned to her *coolie fong*, but she still came to visit us.

As we settled into our new home, I did not dare remind Popo that the 'Muslim devils' had turned out to be our only true friends. All our relatives, Chinese friends and Popo's *chimui*, who had happily accepted our hospitality in the past, had pretended they didn't know about our plight. Some came to visit, and Popo and Mother treated them as if nothing had happened and never mentioned how badly they had let us down or the kindness of Muslim strangers.

I knew Orchard Road quite well: at weekends, Father had often taken Miew-kin and me for walks along it to window-shop or eat *dim sum*. When we came to car showrooms, we would point out the models we wanted to buy for Father. 'I'll buy that great big Ford for you, Papa,' I would shout, and Miew-kin would wave at another and say, 'I'll buy him that big red one.' My father would join in: 'I'll take both and you two can be my drivers.'

Miew-kin and I were seldom rivals and we stuck up for each other whenever we could, but after Father died my sister turned to Mother, craving affection and trying to please her. She never ran away from Mother's rages and didn't even protect her head when Mother hit her. All I could do was listen to her cries as Mother banged her head against the wall. But, no matter how severe the beating, Miew-kin never sulked, and after she had dried her tears, she would be looking at Mother adoringly. Miew-kin not only stopped confiding in me: she began to tell tales to Mother. I could no longer trust even her.

Gasbag Wong still visited us, always on the lookout for a profit. She often brought jade bangles, trinkets and small antiques to sell, hoping to earn a commission. During one of her visits, I overheard snatches of conversation about our *muichai*, Yan-fok.

Mother was saying, 'I've fed and clothed her for nearly six years. How can you imagine that that would be enough for a virgin?'

'You're always complaining that she's stupid and deaf, and you'd be glad to get her off your hands,' Gasbag Wong claimed. 'I didn't tell them any of that. If I had they wouldn't have wanted her for free!'

'So, you're taking advantage because you know I need money for Lim,' Mother said.

That day Gasbag Wong came and went many times. Very early the next morning, at about six o'clock, a woman I had never seen before, carrying a dress-box and accompanied by Gasbag Wong, arrived at our house. Mother took them to her room, called Yan-fok and shut the door.

Minutes later I heard Yan-fok cry, 'No! I don't want to go. I don't want to marry the man in this picture. He's so old, and he's a trishaw-rider.'

Mother's reply was a few hard slaps. A moment later I heard the familiar swish of the cane. 'You'll marry him or be sold to a brothel like Ah-pin. And you know what will happen to you there,' she threatened.

Some time later they all came downstairs. Yan-fok was wearing a hired white bridal gown with her hair nicely done and a headdress of tiny white flowers, but tears ran down her rouged cheeks. She carried a bundle of clothes and I realized she wouldn't come back to our house. Mother called us outside, where several trishaws were waiting to take us to the wedding. One was painted red and this was for the bride and Gasbag Wong, the go-between. Popo was too ill to attend and had asked one of her *chimui* from the temple to go in her place.

It was all so sudden and strange, but when we arrived at the groom's house we saw that an altar had been prepared with many lighted candles and burning joss sticks. An elderly couple in fine Chinese costume sat in armchairs near it. My mother told us later that they were the parents of the groom and had waited a long time to find a wife for their son because they had only just raised the money to pay for the arrangements. Yan-fok and her husband-to-be knelt at the altar and kowtowed many times before heaven, then turned to the old couple and did it again.

Yan-fok was handed a bottle of rice wine to serve to the guests. Gasbag Wong was at her side while she performed the ritual, and afterwards a simple home-cooked meal was served. My mother looked at it. 'The most economical Chinese wedding I have ever attended,' she said.

That night, in the loft with Miew-kin and Wang-lai, I missed Yan-fok, but I was glad she no longer had to endure Mother's beatings. I thought of how we had laughed and talked in the dark until we had fallen asleep. I got up, crept to the corner where she had slept and touched her pillow.

Barely ten days after her wedding, Yan-fok was returned to us by her in-laws. Their son had died in his sleep. They said she had brought them bad luck.

Popo had mellowed after Father's death, and I thought that perhaps she felt guilty about how she had treated him. In fact, her health was failing and she spent much of her time in bed, taking little interest in what went on around her. Soon she was coughing blood. As a herbalist, she continued to prescribe for herself, and we children made the potions and fed them to her – Mother was always busy with Lim. The herbal brews had no effect on Popo's health and, on Mother's order, Miew-kin left our attic to care for Popo, sleeping in the same bed and massaging her for hours every day. She became Popo's handmaid, and hardly went outdoors for so much as a breath of fresh air.

On 15 August 1945, we heard that Japan had surrendered. Our new neighbours had always seemed aloof, never smiling or nodding when I met them in the street, but that day we heard vigorous knocking, and opened the door to see their faces wreathed in smiles. They told us that throughout the occupation they had listened secretly to the news on their wireless and were so terrified of discovery that they had not dared to befriend us. 'The Americans dropped atomic bombs on Hiroshima and Nagasaki!' they gasped.

So, the Japanese silkworms were to be expelled from the Lion City to crawl back across the sea. As we celebrated we wondered if our Japanese neighbours in Paterson Road had packed their gleaming swords.

In the days that followed, the value of Japanese currency fell sharply – we began to call it 'banana money'. Disputes between customers and shopkeepers over price rises were commonplace and I found it an ordeal to shop for the family. There were eight to feed in our household now, not counting Popo's *chimui* who, because of our hospitality when my father was alive, had taken it for granted that they could stay for meals again. In spite of haggling and arguing at the market, I sometimes returned with little food. Mother would accuse me of stealing the money and search me.

In September, Popo's health worsened until her eyes were two deep hollows and the outline of her body hardly showed beneath her thick blankets. She was still coughing blood and was unable to get out of bed to use the toilet. Miew-kin was out of her depth so Mother persuaded one of Popo's *chimui* to live with us and look after her. She was small and hunched, with a friendly face, and older than Popo, in her seventies. We called her Yee Poh, which means grandaunt, and became fond of her as she was kind and gentle.

With the arrival of Yee Poh Miew-kin was free, but not before she had caught tuberculosis from Popo.

Twenty-four

Although Popo was unable to get out of bed, she received a constant stream of visitors from the temple and other friends dropped in nearly every day. Meng-lee came regularly: he cycled all the way from his home in Geylang to sit with her and, knowing how much she enjoyed card games, played rummy with her for hours. Meng-lee had a dark complexion and many remarked that he looked more Malay than Chinese. I liked him because he let me ride his gleaming Raleigh bicycle.

Father's bicycle, which was also a Raleigh but a cheaper model, had been given to my brother after his death as he was the eldest son and Mother thought he should have it. It was not old but it had seen a lot of use. After Beng had spent many hours repairing, cleaning and polishing it, he told me, 'It's mine now, Miew-yong. You can't ride it any more.'

'Why not? What harm will I do it?' I asked. 'I rode it while Father was alive.'

'My friends don't share their bicycles with their sisters. Why should I share mine with you?'

'But I need it for shopping.'

'We aren't buying much now. You can walk,' he said. 'Anyway, Mother will believe anything I tell her about you, so you'd better not touch it.'

I shrugged. I knew that if he let me ride it he would lose face with his new friends. They gathered in the small paved garden at the front of our house to talk about bicycles: which was the best brand, who had the most accessories and how fast you could ride on dirt tracks without getting a puncture. Now that he had emerged from the cocoon of Popo's mollycoddling, my brother, surprisingly, was at ease with other boys. He had my father's amiable nature, but he would not think twice about telling tales to Mother or hitting me when I stood up to him.

After the surrender of the Japanese, Singapore was once more under colonial rule, but everyone welcomed the return of British rule as 'The Liberation'. Orchard Road was busy with British soldiers in military trucks, splashing through the puddles on their way to and from their barracks in Tanglin, a few miles from our house. Whenever I borrowed Meng-lee's bicycle, I wheeled it to the quieter side-streets, then spent a couple of hours riding on narrow lanes and across fields. I was still drawn to our old house in Paterson Road, though, and one day I decided to take a chance on the busy main road and ride past it. As the military vehicles sped by I became nervous, but I could not turn back because that meant crossing the busy road. When I turned left into Grange Road, which was quiet and bordered on both sides by wasteland, shrubs and tall grass, I began to relax. Then, coasting downhill, I heard a vehicle behind me and looked over my shoulder to see a brown military truck approaching at high speed. I was not alarmed as nothing was coming in the opposite direction and the driver had plenty of space to pass me, but I rode as close as I could to the verge.

The next thing I knew I was opening my eyes to find myself tangled with the bike in the ditch. As I struggled to sit up, I realized that the truck had hit me. My legs and elbows were scratched and bleeding and I wondered how long I had lain there. I looked up at the sky: it was not yet midday because the sun was not directly overhead so I knew I had been unconscious for only a short time. I tried to move, but the sloping ditch was covered with thorns and thick undergrowth and I was stuck. I began to shout for help in the hope that someone walking by would hear me.

I was hoarse when it crossed my mind that few people walked along this stretch of road as there were no shops or houses for some distance. I struggled to my feet, felt dizzy and sat down again. My dress was spattered with blood but I thought no bones were broken so I set about freeing the bicycle from the undergrowth. I stared at the twisted rear wheel and remembered that it was not my father's bicycle. It belonged to Meng-lee. Horror drove away the dizziness and fear flooded me. What could I do? I was no longer afraid of Popo – these days, she had hardly the strength to hold a cup of tea to her lips, let alone lift a cane. But I feared Mother's temper: I knew she wouldn't listen to any explanations. I decided to get the bicycle repaired, at any cost, and take it home before Meng-lee left that evening.

The twisted wheel meant that it took a long time to get the bicycle to the repair shop. No one offered to help me on the way, and when the repairman had looked at the damage he said he needed a day to put it right. 'But I have to give it back this evening,' I said, and told him what would happen to me if I did not. My pleas fell on deaf ears. I panicked. My mother would be furious when she saw what had happened to it. I glanced wildly around the shop and saw seats, handlebars and wheels in a rack high above the counter. 'How long would it take to fit that new wheel?' I asked.

'Not very long,' the man said. 'But a new Raleigh wheel is expensive and you must pay me before I do it.'

I had to raise the money. I left the shop, promising to return with the right amount, and ran all the way home. I walked past the dining room where Popo and Meng-lee were playing cards, and hurried up to the loft. No one paid any attention to my bruises and muddy, bloodstained clothes. I counted every cent of my savings to discover I had barely half the amount I needed. I was tempted to borrow from my family, but I knew there would be a string of questions to answer, and if I didn't lie convincingly enough, the accident would be discovered. My mind raced. How could I get hold of the rest of the money? I thought first of Sum-chay. She had a soft spot for us children and sometimes took us to festivals near her *coolie fong* in Hock Lam Street, not far from the Capitol cinema. I knew vaguely where she lived, but hadn't time to search for her. Then I remembered Irene, the Eurasian woman for whom I sometimes babysat.

She lived just fifteen doors away. She had lost her husband in the early days of the invasion and had found work in a nightclub, where she played the piano and sang haunting English and Malay songs. She was tall, with long curly hair. She wore a black or scarlet evening gown to work and looked elegant in her diamanté-studded high-heeled shoes. She had two daughters, a little younger than I was, and a son, Roy, who was about three. She had given her daughters Malay pet names from the songs she sang. The older was Bulan (Moon) and the younger

Bintang (Star). When I passed her house, I could some-times hear her practising the piano and she had taught me a couple of Malay tunes, which I played with two fingers. Whenever she needed me for babysitting, I dropped everything and flew to her house because I would be able to play the piano.

Irene was always kind, and when she opened the door, she was clearly appalled at the state of me. 'What hap-pened? You look –' Irene took my hand and led me to the kitchen. 'Did your mother do this?' she asked. 'Come, let me see how bad it is.' She began to dab at the scratches with cotton wool. I tried to explain that I was in a terrible hurry but she interrupted. 'You can tell me all about it while I clean you up.'

She washed the cuts with warm water, applied a brown tincture that stung, then bandaged my knees and elbows while I told her about the accident and what would hap-pen to me if Mother found out about the bicycle. Irene knew my mother's vicious temper and understood at once why I did not dare ask my family for help. She agreed to give me the money in exchange for a month's babysitting.

I hurried back to the bicycle shop, then waited while two repairmen fitted the new wheel. After a polish, no one could tell that the bicycle had been in an accident and I pushed it home carefully.

Popo and Mother never found out about the accident, but a few weeks later I came close once again to losing my life. I woke one morning to hear anxious voices in the dining room. I jumped up, climbed down from the loft and put my head over the banister to see what was going on. Yee Poh was sitting on Popo's bed, waving her hands. 'The house is flooded,' she cried. 'What shall we do?'

'I'm wet,' Popo complained.

The ground floor was under water. Popo's mattress and several boxes, some containing my father's books and our photo albums, were soaked. The spittoon had overturned and was floating on its side. A carton filled with statues of Buddha and Kuan Yin, sandalwood and joss-stick burners had spilled its contents into the water. Popo had fallen ill before she could ask the *feng-shui* master to advise on the best time, date and position to set up the altar in our new house. Now all of those precious things were contaminated with the contents of the spittoon and muck from the street.

It had rained all night but we had not known that the house was prone to flooding. Popo was too frail to walk so we carried her upstairs where my mother took off her wet clothes, washed her and made her comfortable on Beng's bed. When she was settled we cleared up downstairs as far as we could. We threw away Popo's mattress and pillows, the photo albums, the altar goods and most of my father's books, which he had carefully stamped 'Lum Poh-mun Library'. I opened one to find that the stamp had been blurred by the water, and tears stood in my eyes.

Then, there was nothing to do but wait for the rain to stop and the flood to subside. At the front window I watched cars and people struggle through the water. The monsoon drain had overflowed and the narrow slab bridge from our house to the road was under water. I watched as wooden boxes, branches and coconut seedlings were swept along. Gangs of boys – I recognized some from the *kampung* – were pushing stalled cars. When a vehicle driving down the hill from Tanglin Road slowed to pick its way through the flood, they followed it and sloshed water into the exhaust pipe to kill the engine. Then they crowded round the driver and offered to push it for payment. A white MG sports car pulled up in front of our house. The sound of its powerful engine revving captured the boys' attention and all eyes turned towards it. I recognized the man at the wheel: he had carried out civil-defence duties alongside my father and had visited us at Paterson Road.

He saw me at the window and did not get out but pointed to the flooded road and beckoned me to him. I went to the door and he called that he had brought something for us from Singapore Cold Storage. It was the largest grocery on the island and sold mainly imported Western foods. Its customers had been mostly Europeans, but at Christmas before the war, Father had taken Miewkin and me there to buy presents for his European friends. When we saw the sweets and chocolates our eyes lit up and lingered on the display. We did not ask for anything, but Father bought each of us an oval tin of hazelnut chocolates.

To reach the car I had to leave the house and walk across the drain. I hesitated, then decided to go inside and ask my mother what I should do. Perhaps she would like to go herself, have a chat with Father's friend and thank him for his gift. I found her and Beng sitting on the bed with Popo, all three playing cards. Mother glanced at me with a look that told me not to interrupt. I left the room without saying anything.

Outside, the water was still rushing by. I stepped on to the pavement, feet bare. The water came to just below my waist. I felt unsteady. Cautiously I inched my way forward, toes feeling for the edge of the bridge across the drain. The current pushed against me, and debris forced me to stop half-way. I wanted to turn back but I knew how thrilled everyone would be to receive a gift from Singapore Cold Storage so I pressed on. At that moment I wished I had learnt to swim. Eventually I reached the car and Father's friend handed me a paper carrier-bag that contained a box of Nestlé milk chocolates, a pound of butter and two fresh loaves of bread.

I thanked him, and watched him drive away to make sure that the enterprising car-pushers did not tamper with the MG's exhaust.

I made my way back to the bridge across the drain and, holding the carrier-bag above my head, hurried across. But my mind was on the chocolates so I lost my balance and fell into the drain. Not far away it went underground, and I was carried along in the torrent, unable to stop. As I spun in the water, my head hit something. Dazed, I relaxed and stopped struggling, content to whirl to wherever the water took me.

Suddenly a hand grabbed my arm and, through the water, I saw a man's face. He was wearing glasses and smiling. 'You're safe,' he said, and pulled me out of the water on to the ground, then guided me to a seat in a nearby coffee shop.

A crowd of onlookers gathered round to ask what had happened. When I raised my head, my rescuer was nowhere to be seen. 'Where is he?' I asked.

'Who?'

'My father. Didn't you see him pull me out of the water?'

'*Gila*,' muttered a girl from the *kampung*, who had attended the same school as me. She circled a finger at her temple; she thought I was crazy.

The wife of the coffee-shop owner brought me a hot drink, sat across the table and began to scold me. 'You should know better than to swim in the flood. People have drowned in fast-flowing water.' She went on and on, naming children in the area who had lost their lives playing in the flood.

'I wasn't swimming – I can't swim!' I protested.

'Yes, yes, you can't swim,' she said, humouring me, perhaps. She laid a hand on my shoulder. 'I'll take you home. Where do you live?'

I was glad that she hadn't recognized me because I didn't want Mother to find out about this. 'Let me rest here for a while,' I said. 'I know how to get home.' I finished the drink and she said, 'I'll make you another,' then disappeared into the kitchen.

I left before she came back to ask more questions or, worse, recognize me. From the coffee shop I hugged the walls and gates of my neighbours' houses until I got home. I went up to the loft in my drenched clothes, changed them, then went to Beng's room and sat down to watch the card game.

If my family had found out about the lost food parcel I would have been in trouble. More importantly, I couldn't let my mother find out about the incident lest she accuse me of trying to frighten her by imagining that Father had rescued me. As I watched the cards my mind was still on him. When I was in bed 'You're safe' ran through my mind. The week before I had put my lucky escape down to chance. Now I was sure that my father's spirit had protected me.

The next morning I wanted to talk to someone about what had happened but there was nobody I could trust or who would believe me. I knew they would say that my imagination was playing tricks on me. As I sat miserably in the loft, I remembered that when we lived between the two cemeteries Popo had consulted a medium if she wanted to appease the spirits of the dead or the demons who came out after dusk to roam free in the upper world. She had often taken me with her and now I resolved to go on my own.

I arrived at the dimly lit ground-floor cubicle in Chinatown, clutching some joss sticks, removed my shoes, placed them by the door, then climbed the three steps into a spotlessly clean, incense-filled room. Inside, a small figure sat on the floor, head bowed, legs crossed. Deep in prayer, she was chanting softly. Si Mo frightened me a little. She was old and tiny, no more than four feet tall, and her skin was wrinkled. Popo had told me that her long black hair had never been dyed yet age had not turned even one hair white. Now it was twisted and tied in a knot on the crown of her head and secured so tightly that it lifted the corners of her eyes and brows so that she resembled a warrior in a Chinese opera.

I went quietly towards the altar, where scented flowers, fruit and the statues of many gods were displayed. A large effigy of the medium's most venerated deity, the monkey god, stood in the centre. As I looked into its painted eyes I thought of Grandmother Kum Tai, who had shot the monkey god with her rifle and seen it bleeding at her feet with its hands clasped in prayer. I wondered whether the monkey god was vengeful.

When I had placed the lighted joss sticks on the altar I sat on the floor and waited. I knew I shouldn't disturb a medium in meditation.

When the chanting stopped, Si Mo asked, 'Your Popo didn't come?'

I lied. I said that because Popo was unwell she had asked me to come instead.

'She is not well so she sent you,' the medium mur-mured, as if she were talking to herself.

I felt that she knew I had lied, but her eyes told me nothing.

'Everything has happened so fast in the last two months,' I said, and told her about Father's death, Popo's illness, and how my father had returned to save me from drowning.

'Why are you here?' she asked.

'Popo told me that you can speak to the dead,' I said. 'Please would you talk to my father?' I waited anxiously for her reply.

She left the room and returned with a small charcoal stove, which she placed carefully on a tile to protect the wooden floor. The stove was alive with embers that glowed red and orange. She placed an earthen pot half filled with water on it and settled down. She started to chant prayers, readying herself to go into a trance. As the water came to the boil, the chanting stopped. She plunged her right hand into the bubbling water and called my father's name three times, then asked, 'Have you a message for your daughter?'

She kept her hand in the boiling water, circling it slowly round the pot. Her head swayed from side to side as she said, 'Yesterday was the second time you put your life in danger. Being reckless is not the way to overcome sorrow.'

It was the medium who spoke, but it was my father's way with words. My skin tingled with excitement and fear as I felt his presence. I knew he understood the loneliness and turmoil that had possessed me since he had gone.

Si Mo spoke again: 'Don't be defeated by sorrow.

Remember what I used to tell you when you were unhappy? That will give you strength.' She withdrew her hand from the scalding water and came out of her trance.

Father had often recited sayings to me when he saw my distress at Popo and Mother's ill-treatment, and as I walked home I remembered one in particular that he had liked: 'One must practise everything in moderation. Neither in sorrow nor in happiness should one go to extremes.' Now it comforted me, and I resolved to try to live wisely, as my father had done, and to try to believe, as he had, that human nature tends towards good rather than evil.

I have no doubt that he rescued me from the flood that day, and that he was watching over Miew-kin as well: during a routine medical check-up the doctors discovered her tuberculosis and were in time to cure her completely.

Twenty-five

The relationship between my mother and Lim blossomed. Like a pair of young lovers, they snuggled close on the sitting-room sofa, talking and laughing, oblivious to our glances of disgust.

'People aren't blind. They're talking about you,' Popo said to Mother. 'You're chasing a young man before your husband is cold in the grave.'

But Mother was madly in love. 'I don't care what people say. Let them talk. I can do as I like,' she replied defiantly.

If anyone else dared mention it, she would fly into a rage, hurl a string of obscenities at them, and anything else that came to hand. She threw a barrage of objects at me because she didn't like the way I looked at Lim, the man who had taken my father's place.

'At least you should be more discreet,' Popo scolded her, 'both of you, touching hands and legs in front of the children and visitors.'

Yee Poh, who was old-fashioned and remembered my father fondly for his kindness, was embarrassed, and angry that we children were exposed to my mother's behaviour. 'There is a time and place for such things,' she said.

With Popo ill and my mother besotted with Lim, Yee Poh felt sorry for us. The mention of Father's name brought tears to her eyes. She would say, 'Murderers and arsonists wear belts of gold but menders of bridges and roads have no memorial.' Anyone would have thought from her expressions of grief that she had been his relative, rather than Mother or Popo.

After Popo had remarked on her behaviour, my mother took Lim to her room when he visited and locked the door. If he arrived at a mealtime, she prepared a tray and took it upstairs. I tried to keep out of her way but I found it harder every week to ignore what she was doing: the Japanese army had left so Lim had lost his job at the club and was at our house more often now, sometimes staying overnight.

His wife had discovered that he was involved with my mother and sometimes stood outside on the pavement with her children, calling for him. On those occasions he would leave by the back door to avoid them, but when Miew-kin or I went out Mrs Lim spat at us and we had to run past her to avoid it.

My mother's liaison with Lim had added to our financial problems. Father's Muslim friends, who had offered us the house in Anderson Road, had been giving us money, but when they found out that my mother had lied about the house exchange, they stopped the hand-outs and accused her of taking them for fools. Mother was desperate for money because she had to keep her lover happy so, one by one, our few pieces of carved furniture were sold to antiques dealers.

Lim arrived as my mother was leaving on an errand one day, and decided to wait for her in the sitting room. Sai-ngau ran in to see him, tripped and one of his slippers flew off and hit Lim's head. He was furious, because he believed, like many others, that it would bring him years of bad luck. Miew-kin and I were preparing the evening meal when we heard Lim shouting and raced into the room in time to see him lunge at Sai-ngau, catch him by the scruff of the neck and begin to slap him. No matter how hard Sai-ngau struggled to get away and protested that it had been an accident, Lim would not let him go. His face was bruised and I threatened to call the police if he did not put him down – 'They were my father's friends and you'll go to prison,' I cried.

Lim gave my brother a last slap and pushed him away roughly. 'How dare you threaten me? Wait until your mother comes home. She'll deal with you.' He ran up the stairs, two at a time, to her room and slammed the door.

When Mother returned, she looked in on Popo, then went up to her room. Half an hour later she came down. 'Go into the sitting room, Miew-yong,' she ordered me.

I walked in and she locked the door. My heart sank. There was no escape. From her face, I knew that Lim had told her I had threatened to report him to the police. She didn't ask me what had happened, just caught hold of my dress and tore it. Then, gripping my hair with one hand, she hit me with the other, working herself into a frenzy, punching and slapping me as though she were demented. 'How dare you insult the man I love?' she screamed. 'Where were your manners? I'm going to teach you a lesson you'll never forget.'

'I hate him because he hit Sai-ngau!' I yelled back. 'He will never take my father's place.'

Mother hit me with all her strength and hurled me against the wall. I fell to the floor where she kicked me, then sat on my stomach. She grabbed my hair with both hands and began to bang my head on the floor, screaming, 'I should have strangled you when your father died.'

'Why didn't you?'

She thrust me aside and ran to the cupboard under the stairs. I heard her open the biscuit tin that contained her sewing things and knew she had gone for the scissors. Terror gave me strength. I fixed my eyes on the weapon in my mother's raised hand, but before she could stab me I grabbed her arm and sank my teeth into her hand. I did not let go until she had dropped the scissors. As she bent down to pick them up, I kicked them under the sofa. She straightened up, wringing her hand and cursing me. Then she snatched my father's glass-framed photograph from the wall and smashed it over my head, pulled out the picture, tore it into shreds and flung them into my face. As she slammed out of the room any love I might still have had for her was extinguished.

As Mother and Lim continued their affair, Popo became sicker. The frail figure lying on the bed was a pitiful sight, and now when I looked at her, I found it hard to believe that she had once been so spiteful and cold-hearted. I knew she did not have much time left but I hoped that she would help me understand why she had made my father's life so wretched. I lingered by her bed when she was awake, expecting her to express regret for all the terrible things she had done. But I waited in vain.

One night, I heard her coughing, and when I went into her room the next morning I saw a red blanket pulled over her face. Yee Poh was beside her on a chair, singing sad songs in ancient Chinese, which I did not understand. Her lament went on for hours. When I took her food she refused to eat and I felt sorry for her, but I did not grieve for Popo.

Popo had died three months after my father. Now that Singapore had returned to British rule, everything was in disarray and businesses would not accept Japanese money.

We had no savings in Straits Settlements currency and could not pay for the funeral. My mother had a hard time persuading the undertakers to take the body and had to promise that we would pay with Straits money or it would have been left to decay in the house.

Then we walked four miles from our home in Orchard Road to the funeral parlour in Sago Lane, at the heart of Chinatown, to carry out the wake. We went past the old two-storey terraced houses that lined both sides of the narrow alley, with shops on the ground floor and living quarters above, until we reached the funeral parlours, among the laundries, coffee houses, fishmongers, grocers, butchers, boutiques, joss-paper shops and restaurants.

From dawn until midday, there was an outdoor market in Sago Lane, crowded with itinerant hawkers who brought their goods in large rattan baskets hung on bamboo poles. In the evenings, food stalls opened to serve those arriving to pay their respects to the dead. Even past midnight, crowds thronged the streets, filling the air with the din of conversation. The combination of food stalls, shops and undertakers was a bizarre attraction for foreign tourists. At the funeral parlours the corpses, faces un-covered, were laid out on narrow wooden tables, and beside each there was a vase for joss sticks that were lit by mourners. As people passed each other in the narrow aisles between the bodies, they could hardly avoid the feet of the deceased.

Families kept the joss sticks burning twenty-four hours a day. To stop them falling asleep – which was not in the interests of the food-sellers – there were tables on the pavement for card games and *mah-jongg*. The atmos-phere was not eerie or solemn: everyone behaved as if it was a social event rather than an occasion of mourning, but by midnight the friends had left and only the family stayed on.

To begin with, my mother and Lim stayed beside Popo's body and played *mah-jongg* with other mourners during the night. Aunt Chiew-foong made only short visits during the day, saying she could not leave her children for long. Beng, Miew-kin, Yan-fok and I devised a rota to keep the joss sticks burning from morning to midnight. Yee Poh needed a rest: she had been up all night caring for Popo over the past few days and was exhausted. She wasn't well enough to make the eight-mile round trip to and from Chinatown and remained at home with Wang-lai and Sai-ngau.

There was still the problem of money to pay for the funeral so my mother appealed to my aunt and a few close friends for loans. She hoped they would help as our family had helped them during the hard times of the Japanese occupation. But everyone said they had no savings in Straits money and her hopes faded. Time was running out and she was getting desperate. She hadn't the energy to spend the day trying to raise the money and then stay up all night keeping vigil beside Popo's corpse. Somebody else would take on that unpleasant task.

'Sago Lane is not a good place for Beng in the small hours. Miew-kin has been ill and dozes off easily,' Mother said, so it was Yan-fok and I who would stay from midnight until seven in the morning. 'The joss sticks must burn continuously,' my mother warned, so Yan-fok and I kept a close eye on them. I wished Popo's body had been nearer the entrance: to light the scented joss sticks beside her, I had to walk down the aisle between the two rows of bodies, some of which had maggots crawling on their faces. The bodies were decomposing because the families had no means to pay, and the undertakers would not release the bodies for burial until they had the money. In the tropical heat, the stench of rotting flesh filled the room, despite the scent of the incense.

Three days and three nights passed, and still my mother had not been able to raise the money to bury Popo. As Yan-fok and I sat through the night in the funeral parlour, we became more and more dispirited. On the fourth day maggots appeared on Popo's face, and although the smell of decay was overwhelming and the sight was sickening, I could not take my eyes off them.

Eventually my mother had to tell the undertakers that she hadn't been able to raise any money but, at the eleventh hour, they discovered that as my father had been a government servant he could receive backdated pay from the new colonial government. They finally allowed the funeral to go ahead. Popo was taken from Sago Lane to Pek San Teng cemetery. As she had had no sons, the duty of following the hearse holding a memorial flag fell to Beng, her eldest grandson. My mother was an obedient daughter and wanted to honour her mother so she paid Taoist priests to chant prayers and play musical instruments, and two professional mourners to lament loudly. As the body was lowered into the earth, my only thought was that she would never hurt me again. As my mother sobbed and the mourners wailed, Miew-kin, Yan-fok and I tried to cry because we knew it was expected of us. But no tears came to our eyes and all we could feel was relief that Popo had gone.

After Popo's death my mother was accountable to no one, so it wasn't long before Lim left his family and moved in with us. My brothers and sisters accepted him as their new father, but I couldn't understand how they had forgotten our true father so quickly. For this 'insolence', I was not allowed to sit at the table when Lim made dinner for the family. 'After we have finished, you may have what's left,' my mother would say. But I refused to eat anything that Lim had cooked. Instead, I went out to the garden and picked the sour *belimbing* from our neighbour's tree, which overhung the fence. It gave me stomach-ache and diarrhoea.

We were sent back to English schools, my two brothers to the Anglo-Chinese School, my sisters and I to the Methodist Girls' School. Each morning as we set off, we would find Lim's wife waiting outside. As we walked past she would spit at us, and on our way home she would spring out from doorways and shout at us, attracting curious looks from passers-by. Eventually, we took a detour, and even though it meant walking an extra mile, it was worth it to avoid the scenes.

We had just settled in to the new routine when we were confronted once more with upheaval. Lim had to pay for his son's education and wanted to buy a rambutan plantation. My mother was always worried that he would leave her and tried to raise some money for him. But he needed it quickly and told her to sell the lease on our house in Orchard Road. She did so, with every stick of furniture, including the teak table that had sheltered us from the bombs, the landscape paintings, ornaments, crockery and anything else that people would buy. When she had finished, the house was bare except for her double bed, the kitchen table, some pots and pans, a few stools and our clothes. With the money she had made, she bought Lim the rambutan plantation and rented a shabby two-room *attap* house for us in nearby Orange Grove Road. She and Lim went to live on the plantation. Hock,

Lim's son, was sent to board with a family near his Chinese school in Katong, and my sisters, brothers, Yan-fok and I moved to the *attap* house. It had not been occupied for some time and the roof let in sunlight and rain. There was no electricity or modern sanitation, and a well was the only source of water. Each morning we would draw up the bucket and look in dismay at the algae and weeds.

We were never taken to the plantation and I wondered how my mother felt to be back in the countryside where she had begun her married life with my father, Kum Tai and Fat Lum, whether her new place had a duckpond and what she did about the fruit bats that came out of the night sky to feast on the red rambutans. It wasn't long before she and Lim gave up farming and came to live with us in two cramped rooms. Lim complained constantly about the overcrowding, and whenever there was a flare-up between him and Mother, she took it out on Miew-kin and me.

Not long after they returned, Yan-fok was struck down with severe dysentery. Weak and pale, she was forced to carry the chamber-pot around with her as she worked. My mother couldn't have cared less about how ill she was and left her to suffer until one day Ismail, who had been a neighbour when we were in Paterson Road, dropped in. Ismail was an office boy in a city firm – dark with unruly curly hair and a pimply face. He had befriended Tamby, our gardener, and was often seen chatting to him in our garden. To me, he was no different from the other boys in the *kampung*. I had no notion at that time that he had an eye for Yan-fok. He was appalled at the state Yan-fok was in and took her to hospital. I waited for him to return and tell us how she was but he did not come that day or the next. After a week, I was upset and anxious. I wondered whether she was alive or dead. A few more weeks went by, and there was still no news of Yan-fok, so one afternoon I went to the *kampung* near our old house to look for Ismail, only to discover that he and his family had moved away, no one knew where.

Soon we were moving again, this time to a house in the Cairnhill area. Mother and Lim left us again to run a restaurant by the beach in Bedok, on the east coast of Singapore. Mother returned once a month to pay the rent and leave some money for our food and schooling. We were often hungry but we never let on to friends and neighbours, and our spirits were high. Then she stopped giving us money so we could not pay our fees or buy textbooks. When my teacher, Mrs Salmon, found out that I did not have my own books, she pinched my eyelid and twisted the skin.

Miew-kin was fourteen and I was thirteen when we decided to leave school. We had to earn money to feed Beng, Sai-ngau and Wang-lai and keep them at school. We lied about our ages and found our first jobs as clerks, helping people to fill in the forms and mark them with a thumbprint to get their identity cards. Until then I had always used my Chinese name, but my new friends at the office were of different races and some found it difficult to remember. During our lunch breaks we would stroll down to the food stalls by the banks of the Singapore river and one day someone suggested my sister and I should adopt English names. We decided on Mary for Miew-kin and Lucy for me.

Later on I found a job as a telephonist and Miew-kin was hired as a receptionist at a dry-cleaner's. I was paid ninety-six dollars a month. After I had paid the monthly grocery account of about sixty dollars and the school fees, bought textbooks and provided Beng, Sai-ngau and Wang-lai with pocket money, I had fifteen dollars for myself. At the end of the month I often had nothing, not even for lunch at work.

Although my sister and I worked hard to keep the family, our brothers did not appreciate our efforts. One evening when I had just got home from work, Beng demanded two dollars for a bicycle part. When I told him I didn't have the money he found a copper pipe and ran towards me, brandishing it. I was standing on the steps outside our house and shielded my face as he came towards me. But he ran up a few steps beyond where I was standing, then began to hit me. Sai-ngau, who had been playing nearby, joined in. My brothers had been well taught by Popo and Mother.

Several months went by when Mother didn't even pay the rent, but mercifully Miew-kin earned enough to cover that. Then, as suddenly as they had left, my mother and Lim returned. She told us that we were to give her our wages and she would let us have pocket money to get to work. Every morning Miew-kin and I went out to earn money for our family, Lim and his son, and every evening we returned to face Mother's uncertain temper.

Twenty-six

Two years after the war Kung-kung returned to the news that my father and Popo were dead. My mother lost no time in berating him for walking out on his family. She told him that she had begged his fellow stallholders for news and walked the streets looking for him, then demanded to know where he had been and what he had done.

She served him with bowls of tea in the sitting room and I listened as they talked. Kung-kung told her that when he had sold the herbal-medicine stall and moved out of the family home, he had not left the country at once but had stayed for a few months in nearby Maxwell Road, in a rented room, to make up his mind about what he was going to do. During that time he had met his old friend Chow, who had got him a job aboard his ship. He had returned to Singapore on the ship twice but had not wanted to see his family because Popo had made him lose face. In early 1940 his ship had docked in San Francisco. He and Chow had settled there and set up a laundry for the thousands of servicemen who passed through the port bound for the war. He and Chow's family could not cope with all the washing, scrubbing and ironing, and their hands were so sore and blistered that they had hired six more workers: four Chinese men, the Mexican wife of one and their daughter, Suet-lay.

Suet-lay was in her twenties with thick black hair tied with a red ribbon. As Kung-kung spoke of her, his voice was gentle and I could tell that she meant something to him. 'But for her eyes no one could tell her father was Chinese and she spoke Spanish and Cantonese equally well,' he said.

Mother pressed him to tell her more and he said he had paid her no attention at first and treated her like any of his other workers. But when he had scalded his hands while he was stirring towels in boiling soda water, Suet-lay had looked after him. She had bandaged his hands and fed him at mealtimes when he could not hold his chopsticks. He had become close to her. As he spoke I was surprised to see that he was holding back tears. Mother noticed this, too, and urged him to tell her everything. After a long sigh, he told her sadly that he had raised another family with Suet-lay in 'the gold mountain', as he called San Francisco. He had two more daughters but, still, no son. 'They are very young,' he said. 'Lian-fa is four and Mei-fa is three. I would have stayed for a son but they will be well provided for with my share of the laundry. Maybe I'll go back and see them some day.'

Kung-kung returned to his flat in Tanjong Pagar Road and lived in the same room he had shared with Popo. He spent a few cents each day on pressed tofu and vegetables, and even worked part-time in a coffee shop. He didn't need to because he had an income from the rooms he let and had saved a lot of his earnings from working in the ship's laundry, but he disliked being idle and, even more, spending money. I once heard him boast to my mother and Aunt Chiew-foong that he was well off: 'I have gold coins, many pieces of expensive jewellery and a fat bank account.' On one of our visits to the flat he took us children into his room, pulled out a big wooden trunk from under his bed and showed us the coins and jewellery. 'When I am gone,' he said, 'all this will be divided between my grandchildren.'

After his two daughters learnt of his wealth, they competed for his attention. One day when we visited him, Lim came too, hoping for his approval, but the two men said not one word to each other and, later, Kung-kung said many angry ones to my mother for having chosen a younger, married man. 'You must never bring him here again,' he told her. My aunt, unlike my mother, was patient and knew how to take advantage of the rift that had grown between Kung-kung and his elder daughter. Her father was old-fashioned and respected people with government connections. I heard her remind him many times that her husband worked for the government. Before long Kung-kung and Cong had become close, much to my mother's displeasure.

The years at sea had cured his addiction, but Kung-kung continued to visit an opium den and, in time, the reason for his visits became clear. I overheard my mother telling my aunt that he was seeing a woman who worked there, and his tenants had told her that he was less grumpy at home and even joked with them. Aunt Chiew-foong said she would visit the opium den herself to learn more about the woman and try to rake up some of her history to put fire in Kung-kung's ears. She and my mother were united against a common enemy who, they feared, would stand between them and the chest of riches that was kept under Kung-kung's bed.

Soon after we found out about Kung-kung's new woman friend he invited us to celebrate his birthday and we gathered at his flat for dinner. My family, my aunt's family and the tenants sat at three round tables on the landing next to the altar, where the walls were sooty with the smoke from a thousand joss sticks. When we were all comfortable Kung-kung disappeared into the bedroom, then reappeared with a small, dainty woman wearing a silk *samfoo* and jewellery on her wrists and fingers. Her hair was arranged in two plaits and decorated with jade and pearl hairpins. They walked towards the tables and I realized that my family and the tenants must have been expecting to see Kung-kung with her because they had glasses in their hands ready to toast them. My aunt exchanged a sour look with my mother.

'This is Choy-ying,' Kung-kung said, and presented her to them. Then he turned to us children: 'This is your new grandmother,' he said.

In honour of his birthday, Kung-kung had, as usual, replaced the dim lightbulbs with brighter ones. I was glad of the chance to study Choy-ying. She spoke little and smiled often and, as I watched her eating, I thought about my other grandmothers, gentle Kum Tai, whom I had never known and who had shot the monkey god by mistake, and Popo, who had forbidden Kum Tai's son ever to speak her name, and who had tied her granddaughter to a teak table and burnt her lips and eyelids.

Later that year while I was walking on the high street towards the Victoria Memorial Hall, I came across Yan-fok, wearing Malay dress and carrying a baby. She had put on a little weight and looked healthy and contented. I could see the shock on her face when she spotted me, and Ismail seemed embarrassed. Yan-fok hurried towards me and begged me, panic-stricken, not to tell my mother I had seen her. She had a family now, she said, and Ismail drove trucks for the British army. My mother would torture her if she was forced to return to us.

I was angry that she hadn't let me know she was safe and well, after we had been through so much together at the hands of my mother and Popo, but I knew she was right. If Mother found her, she would punish Yan-fok, who would have to return to our house. When I was older, I would be able to escape my mother but Yan-fok, as a *muichai*, would be trapped. I knew I could not betray her and gave her my promise. Yan-fok thanked me and kissed her baby. As I watched her walk away with Ismail, she turned and gave me a wide smile.

Acknowledgements

I would like to thank Peter West Mason for encouraging me to tell my story and for helping me with my English.

PublicAffairs is a publishing house founded in 1997. It is a tribute to the standards, values, and flair of three persons who have served as mentors to countless reporters, writers, editors, and book people of all kinds, including me.

I.F. STONE, proprietor of *I. F. Stone's Weekly*, combined a commitment to the First Amendment with entrepreneurial zeal and reporting skill and became one of the great independent journalists in American history. At the age of eighty, Izzy published *The Trial of Socrates*, which was a national bestseller. He wrote the book after he taught himself ancient Greek.

BENJAMIN C. BRADLEE was for nearly thirty years the charismatic editorial leader of *The Washington Post*. It was Ben who gave the *Post* the range and courage to pursue such historic issues as Watergate. He supported his reporters with a tenacity that made them fearless and it is no accident that so many became authors of influential, best-selling books.

ROBERT L. BERNSTEIN, the chief executive of Random House for more than a quarter century, guided one of the nation's premier publishing houses. Bob was personally responsible for many books of political dissent and argument that challenged tyranny around the globe. He is also the founder and longtime chair of Human Rights Watch, one of the most respected human rights organizations in the world.

For fifty years, the banner of PublicAffairs Press was carried by its owner Morris B. Schnapper, who published Gandhi, Nasser, Toynbee, Truman, and about 1,500 other authors. In 1983, Schnapper was described by *The Washington Post* as "a redoubtable gadfly." His legacy will endure in the books to come.

Peter Osnos, *Founder and Editor-at-Large*